Trilogy:
'He Heals the Broken Hearted'

Children of God

Conformed to The Life-Giving Cross in Joy and Hope in Eternal Life

Marina Carrier

Dedication

To all those, who from my conception, threw me into the Arms of God the Father, and in essence gave me the opportunity to learn to suffer with Christ before I understood Love and Grace.

And to all those who enabled me to open up to know my Truth in Christ, not least four Evangelical Students. They put all fear aside and were obedient to the Holy Spirit to witness to me about Christ's Love and work when I was an Acting Head of Department in a Polytechnic. They persevered in prayer for me, including giving me a prophecy telling me I was 'precious in God's sight' (which I did not believe) and that the waters (emotions) and fire (anger)would not consume me.

(Isaiah 43: 1-9)
And that passage goes on:
"You are my witnesses," declares the LORD,
"and my servant whom I have chosen,
that you may know and believe me
and understand that I am he.
Before me no god was formed,
nor shall there be any after me.
I, I am the LORD,
and besides me there is no saviour.*

So I want to include Clay and Mary McClean, servants of God – bringing Truth and Love through Inner Healing Conferences.

As they taught the Holy Spirit worked in me. So much darkness and evil came to Light as the Truth of God and His Love and Grace in Christ began the revelation of my history, the shame, lies and ways I had covered my pain. And at the same time He revealed through the 'broken' and 'weak' around me, the True Life of Christ, as they reached out to me in compassion, love and support for this broken heart they saw being revealed. I was truly on my journey of repentance, humility and healing.

So dear Heavenly Father, Glorious Son Jesus Christ, and Holy Spirit – I give to You, all You have given me, in witness to You, Your Grace and Love – and follow this calling you gave me in Baptism 80 years ago, then again when you brought me back into the church, 50 years later. To God alone be GLORY.

*'Isaiah is above all else the prophet of faith. He begins to define the quality of faith and what it means to trust in God. It's a whole new capacity for God and life…. Biblical faith, especially for Isaiah, is a quality of being, a quality of perception.'

Adapted from Richard Rohr, The Prophets (San Antonio, TX: Catholic Charismatic Bible Institute, 1980), audio recording. No longer available for purchase.

Acknowledgements

None of this could have been done without the ongoing prayers of the saints in heaven, and on earth. Thank you all.

Thanks too to those who have persevered in helping me regarding the Third Book: Martin Stone, my faithful reader; Andrew Evans – who mirrors a 'sacrificial servant' to me in his willingness to bear the burdens of this process with me; and Carl Denig in encouraging and editing the book. And to Tatiana Villa, for patient and skilful creation of the book cover.

I want to thank God who led me to Indira Hnatiuk and her grace and humility in suffering to find healing solutions through God's leading. Thank you, Indira, for sharing this wisdom and purity...and your willingness to provide so I could learn more of the Truth in 'Strengthening the Inner Being' in faith and Grace. My faith and your 'science' taught by God through overcoming suffering are living witnesses to His Universal Fathering and provision for His servants with Love for His Children.

Preface

This is the Third book of the Trilogy, 'He heals the Broken Hearted'. This one, *'Children of God: Conformed to The Life-Giving Cross in Joy and Hope in Eternal Life'* demonstrates God's on-going work in building and leading me, Marina, into His likeness and service, within the context of life lived in the world.

Dear Reader, I am the first to acknowledge that all is a miracle of answered prayer. Early on in my return to active life in the Church, when someone praying for me realised how 'empty' I was within, she prayed this prayer of St Paul for the Ephesians. I eventually started praying it every day for months, and years and still now when some emptiness reveals itself. **And dear Reader, you can pray it too.**

'For this reason I bow my knees to the Father of our Lord Jesus Christ, from whom the whole family in heaven and earth is named,
that He would grant you, according to the riches of His glory, to be strengthened with might through His Spirit in the inner man,
that Christ may dwell in your hearts through faith;
- that you, being rooted and grounded in love,
may be able to comprehend with all the saints what is the width and length and depth and height—
to know the love of Christ which passes knowledge; that you may be filled with all the fullness of God.
Now to Him who is able to do exceedingly abundantly above all that we ask or think, according to the power that works in us,
to Him be glory in the church by Christ Jesus to all generations, forever and ever. Amen.' Ephesians 3:14-21

While needing to deal with disappointment, life changes and work in the Spirit, I was sustained on this journey in faith, hope and love. I readily invited the Holy Spirit to develop, purify and teach me to serve Him in Spirit and in Truth – then finding joy and hope, thus *'grounding and rooting 'me*, through giving His Love. The book underlines our total dependence on God the Father, through Christ and the Holy Spirit in order:

*to Love and be Loved in purity of heart.
*to act in Grace, rather than through our own effort and minimal understanding;
*to Trust that all our needs will be met – in God's Time;
*to grow in the fruit of the Spirit through praise and patient perseverance;
*and to know that NOTHING can separate us from Christ's Love.. through the Holy Spirit.

But God does things at the right time, preparing our hearts and minds, and those with whom we will relate, learn from and serve. With our human desire for control – we need to surrender to 'Your Will be done', in Your Time!!!

We get to ask the questions, or recognise a need- and He provides- but we need to be open to His provision which may not match our expectation or human desire!! Or other times when, out of the blue, we are blessed with 'more than you can ask or conceive' (Ephesians 3:20)!! And thus we turn another corner or climb steps, or even find Christ's love in the depths. God Provides. We truly are His Children even when we don't consciously recognise Him at work.

This is a personal reflection and account of God's work and provision in my life in Him as I start life afresh in Scotland, after seven plus years working in a parish. **Dear Reader**, Come with me on this new part of the journey. See how God builds, and challenges, this human life, that embodied many of the trials of people today including, at its commencement, the use of children to gratify the sexual desires of adults; and later, overwork and exhaustion when disbelief and lack of trust made turning to man or to God for help no option. See how Marina is gently enabled to make new steps of commitment.

History, in the form of unredeemed memories, interpretation of events, or false beliefs about my responsibilities still needed to be recognised and overcome. Only through the Holy Spirit's purification and my desire and willingness for integration of body,

Soul and Spirit could a greater Good be lived out.

We see how God brought hidden wounds into view, and healed them, and how His Love softens, purifies and redeems a broken heart and life, making a Child of God, confident that nothing separates me from His Love.

Lets go together to end of the journey from Kinston to Scotland......and the beginning of the next step

Introduction

Though your father and mother forget you, I will never forget you', says the Lord

Dear Reader, 'Unless you become like a little child, you cannot enter the Kingdom of God' (Matthew 18:3).

As a child I was powerless in the world, and I suffered from my mother's depression and shame that I was alive, and my step-father's abuse. Yet through baptism I had Love and obedience to the Holy Spirit at work in me, and I sought to be obedient to the leading of the Holy Spirit. Thus, despite neglect at home, through God's mercy I had help to pass exams to get to Grammar School and then get to Teacher Training College. I followed the leading of the Holy Spirit in teaching, and questions were raised in my heart leading to more courses, taking a zig-zag path following the questions.

Despite proclaiming my faith that Christ was the Son of God after doing A level Scripture, I did not follow a route in the traditional church that I had experienced as a child. I simply trust this with God because He knew the childish, subconscious blame for the abuse I put on the church. Yet He was providing Spiritual food because each day in schools at that time, we had 'assembly' which was overtly Christian. I can remember 'yawning' (a form of deliverance) as I (we) prayed the Lord's prayer each day at Assembly.

Thus God taught me and His Spirit encouraged me in school despite my mother's inability to support me. I was given an older boyfriend who took me with him to study at the Reference Library. He taught me how to condense my notes to two pages for each subject at the end of the fourth year which led me to passing seven subjects that I could take at O level in the fifth year!!

Although I was blessed by taking A level Scripture, I only got an O level pass when the exam paper focus (Doctrine in the early church) did not match what we had been studying (Mission/Practice in the early church). Despite this meaning I could not go to University I see God's hand in preparing for me to train as a teacher, after a year of unqualified teaching, teaching me I knew nothing!

In all these events, despite disappointment, I followed guidance from the Headteacher at school. But once qualified, it seemed I was lead by my Heart, despite the undertow of 'loneliness' which at times led to some unwise decisions. So along with my teaching in Secondary Modern, Grammar, Special Needs, Infant and Special schools – I got married – totally ignoring the 'wisdom' of my intuition – my inner-being which was fighting against it. We adopted a son, and spent 7 years in Norfolk.

Like with other things, I persevered in my work, and with the family life, but his unfaithfulness eventually led to divorce, further research study and finally, 'at the top of the tree,' I was without hope or love, as the man I was living with did not want to marry me.

But God still held me- and when exhausted as an Acting Head of Department in a Polytechnic, He called my name and I was brought back into the Body Of Christ in the Church…held in His Love.

After years of my mind, and now my heart, trying to keep the commandments of God, I saw one day in Wells Cathedral, that Christ himself fell with the weight of the Cross. He was given Courage and Strength to get up again and persevere. I could stop beating myself up when the difficulties of life were too heavy for me.

That was when the mercy of God entered my life and I needed to open my heart door to His Love and Grace. At this time a friend was training as a Reader and needed to go to the service of another denomination. She invited me to go with her to the Roman Catholic Church in the village. My heart went 'PING!' when she asked me over the phone!!

This led to my first confession to the Roman Catholic priest who had welcomed my friend and I as visitors to his Palm Sunday Vigil Mass. (As I was sitting at the back during the mass, and I was convicted of spiritual pride: 'These are MY People,' I heard, as I literally felt the 'weight' of God on me as He said these words. I was humbled and repentant.)

The priest had shown us around the church after Mass, including showing us the confessional. It was a modern church so there were no enclosed 'boxes'. However the significant point of the visit for me was the priest's invitation to his parishioners to come in during the following week to do the meditations on the Stations of the Cross. I knew I must do this.

I came in near the beginning of the week, and I took over 3 hours to follow the meditations around the Stations of the Cross. I wept much of the time and knew at the end that I must make confession. I didn't really know what this meant – I just knew what I had to confess. Through the mercy of the priest and the kindness of his housekeeper in finding him, I confessed my hatred of myself as a woman. He could not give the normal 'penances' as I didn't know them but showed me a picture of 'Jesus Light of the World'. This is the Holman Hunt painting of Christ standing outside a door covered in briars, but the only handle is on the inside. This is a representation of our heart door, shut against Christ's Love. He asked me to pray and ask for forgiveness and to open my heart door to let Him in to this hurt.

Indeed – I always was His child. 'Though your father and mother abandon you, I will never leave you, says the Lord" (Psalm 27:10) – but He needed me to grow in Love and mercy. How could I love others if I hated myself as a woman?

But the lies I had lived with, and the shame that I felt because of not being wanted in utero, being born a girl, and then abused for over 4 years, wrapped the Truth in layers of separation from the Beauty and wonder of His Love embracing and filling me. The Truth, sealed through Baptism, was constantly leading and upholding me in goodness and service; and His Truth was wanting to fill me to bursting to tell the world 'what He has done for me'. (Psalm 105) But like an iceberg, there was buried treasure in the dark!!

So here I am – given this awesome task of writing this Trilogy proclaiming to the world, how He heals the Broken-hearted. How through His Love the human soul and mind, may surrender to His Spirit and grace in Love; find all the burdens surrendered; all the striving changed; all the vain-glory and pride melted by love and His desire for the World to be opened to the wonder of His Love and invitation. And daily GROW in choosing for His Spirit over all other 'pleasures' knowing the Joy of 'doing His Will'.

Dear Reader, nothing can separate me, or you, from His Love, because He turns all things to Good through His wisdom, gentleness, and the mystery of His Mercy and Love embodied in Jesus Christ and the Cross and Resurrection. But He does need our 'Yes'.

How can I be His witness as He calls me to? I cannot tell more than I know because I am not God…but I know that when I ask for help to do something He has asked me to do, He gives me answers - not theoretical answers – He shows me what to do, or how to respond, or the way LOVE could be operating in this situation.

Like the time I was given a teaching post in a classroom of special needs children – when I had no training or direct experience of either teaching this age or need. I was led to build up an environment of love and respect – deliberately choosing something I could love about each child, and building a culture of mutual respect and need. I created an educational framework of mornings given to learning reading, writing and maths, etc but the afternoons were for learning games etc. which led to them being able to make choices.

I was led to encourage every child to use their 'gift,' because we all had 'gifts' and we all had needs. Gladys was in charge of tidying my desk!! Thank you Lord for all the ways Gladys provided for me…..

But Dear Reader – what I want to emphasise is the fullness of God's provision when He is providing for our needs…. When we are seeking to serve His desire to build others.

So lets recall this is an introduction – not the full book. Three things to remember:

> 1)   There were many facets of Christ's life (human and divine) and so there are in ours, even when given over to Christ.. and as we grow in Grace, Understanding, Love, so God's call on us to 'witness' grows and changes as St Paul makes clear (1 Corinthians 13:11)..

2)   When we are given and surrendered to Christ, we are 'chosen vessels' (Acts 9:15) whether we remember it or not, and God can move us to the far ends of the earth, or root us in a monastery, or allow us to be a piece of flotsam and jetsam on the sea of life. Whichever way God calls us, we need to keep our eyes on Him and allow every revealed block in our lives to lead us to greater purity of Heart and humility in the Holy Spirit through repentance and surrender....always in Love.. We have NOTHING of eternal value without Him and His Spirit....

3)   We need to grasp Christ's humility before the Father -He waited for 'His time'; He only did 'what He saw the Father doing, or what the Father told him to do' (John 5:19)....And I am constantly made aware of how the Father extended Christ's boundaries and put people before Him, the Samaritan woman (John 4:4-42) and the Syro-Phoenician woman (Mark 7:24-30) for example, who challenged assumptions about those He was called to serve. It was as if the Father wanted Christ to recognize, and remember always, the deep purity of God's Love – that 'in Christ' were no boundaries. And it is significant that with Christ's resurrection, after descending to hell, His final instructions to His disciples were to go to ALL nations to preach the gospel (Matthew 28:19-20).

Dear Reader,
I sense in my Soul and Heart my love/God's Love for you –

May you be blessed as you continue with increasing courage and humility to seek more of His Heart, Mind and Will in your own lives and heart.

'I bow my knees to the Father of our Lord Jesus Christ, that He would grant you, to be strengthened with might through His Spirit in the inner man...'

What follows is the continuation of the prayer of St Paul to the Ephesians which forms the framework of this book. Without surrender to the Father, and prayer for the Holy Spirit and Word of God in Christ, we cannot be Children of God.

For this reason I bow my knees to the Father of our Lord Jesus Christ, from whom the whole family in heaven and earth is named,

that He would grant you, according to the riches of His glory, to be strengthened with might through His Spirit in the inner man,

that Christ may dwell in your hearts through faith; that you, being rooted and grounded in love,

may be able to comprehend with all the saints what is the width and length and depth and height—

to know the love of Christ which passes knowledge; that you may be filled with all the fullness of God.

Now to Him who is able to do exceedingly abundantly above all that we ask or think, according to the power that works in us,

to Him be glory in the church by Christ Jesus to all generations, forever and ever. Amen.

Come Holy Spirit.

Table of Contents

1

Rooted and Grounded in Love
Part One

Let not your heart be troubled; you believe in God, believe also in Me." (John 14:1). Releasing Fear – and Growing in Trust. –

'Strengthen them in their inner being, that Christ may dwell in their hearts by faith…" (Eph 3:14-19) – Growing beyond the rational.

13th October 2021

Here I am alone in the new flat in Prestonpans, Scotland– totally dependent on God. Lord have mercy.

Dear Reader, As a child I had no control over my environment and could not define nor meet my needs. I want to honour God in the way He strengthened me to GROUND me in Love in these first few months in this new dwelling. But I had to be humble before Him for it to happen.

'Unless you become like a little child, you cannot enter the Kingdom of God' (Matthew 18:3).

This latter is a BIG statement. *'It is harder for a rich man to get into the Kingdom, than for a Camel to pass through the eye of a needle'*, says Jesus (Matthew 19:24). There was purportedly a small gateway into Jerusalem which was called 'the eye of the needle'. It was impossible for a loaded camel to get through that door.

And we are like that loaded camel, while we hang on to worldly position, 'image', knowledge, even 'spiritual practises' that we feel are crucial for us to get into the Kingdom; all these block our entrance.

"When the disciples heard this, they were greatly astonished and asked, 'Who then can be saved?' Jesus looked at them and said, 'With man this is impossible, but with God all things are possible.'" (Matthew 19:25-26)

Imagine the camel with all its load removed– it could then bend its knees and even shuffle through the door. It would be like a child, humble, pure and obedient to the Way and the call of God leading from Within and Without, with no pride or vainglory involved.

So in all humility we look to God to enable us receive His Love, and love Him in return with all we are, and thus embrace the humility of a child, to become His Children. Thus, we become *'strengthened in our Inner Being…'*

I had arrived in Scotland to the flat given by God! A six-hour drive had passed, despite the rain, without stress. Most boxes had arrived in the right room for unpacking, after the careful labelling back in Kinston, and the diligent work of the furniture removers. My over-arching feeling as I stood in the new flat, was of unutterable gratitude.

And at the same time I was aware that God was upholding me. My work for Him for the next week at least, was to focus on making the flat habitable and workable. That first night I got my box-bed made up and went early to bed.

Over the next week I walked in wonderment from room to room – feeling SOOO blessed to have room to be alive in the gifts He had given….and so blessed to have the living room and my studio/bedroom overlooking the sea. (AT times at high tide when I looked out of the left-hand window of the living room, it looked as if we were IN the sea.)

This three-floor building was built on a rock on the beach. Normal high tides simply covered the beach in front, and to the left of us up to the sea wall, which kept the sea from the High Street and main road. At 'springs' high tides, particularly accompanied by strong winds, the waves even hit my balcony doors and threatened to take whatever was on the balcony!! I was on the 1st floor – with a flat below me and one above.

So alongside the wonder and contentment of the views, I was also given Grace to see one thing at a time that needed doing to create order, and on completion of that thing, I would know what was next. Thus, I was never overwhelmed, nor did my strength fail till I needed rest at night!

Piece by piece the furniture found a home and purpose, and books, stationery, art materials and computer were gradually restored to order on shelves in appropriate rooms or on the allotted desk. And M came to fit blinds in kitchen and bedroom, and curtain poles in other rooms on which re-made curtains were hung on old curtain rings. (I gratefully recalled the donors.)
In time M was also able to install the clothes airer and the 'wardrobe unit', in the narrow storeroom. I was so grateful for both these.

I was aware that my son and his wife had 'booked' an anniversary weekend in my Prestonpans flat in November for their 25th Wedding Anniversary. I needed to make provisions. This was made via the local 'junk' yard- though the two mattresses were almost new. They arrived a week before needed.

Dear Reader – No words can express my gratitude to God for the gift of this flat and even the prompting to make St Chad the covering saint. He was present at the front door which was accessed from the outside steps at the side of the building near the beach. It made me even more determined and loving towards God's purposes.

Every morning was an inordinate gift as I opened the blinds to see where and how the tide was…very fierce with many breakers or still and gentle, even hardly moving on the surface? And with the different tides came different birds.

I truly felt 'parented by God' and sensed His provision for my soul, 'hidden in Christ, in God'. Here I was truly being 'grounded' in love in all ways, as the internet connection finally was in place, and I became established with a doctor's surgery, and a dentist. I even got my funeral plan changed to function in Scotland for no additional cost.

I was receiving time to overcome deeper abandonment of my soul and Spirit by facing, in Christ, a situation of safety, and without constant change of expectation. Remember dear Reader, I had found solace by 'serving' as it covered ancient pain and loss, yet many times in the last few years Jesus had made it clear I was being a 'prostitute' because I was agreeing to do what others wanted, NOT what God was wanting or needing of me deep in my soul. 'Be still and know that I am God' (Psalm 46:10).

So I was in this situation, clearly God's provision, which fed my soul, but definitely not 'serving' in any overtly visible way or as I had for the last seven years:

Had Christ abandoned me? Was I still God's child? This is the question the Lord wants me to address because there are many today who suffer/suffered abuse by parents, and subsequently lose faith when they are not overtly doing what others have asked them to do.

Firstly: God carried me through the early years and provided for me in other ways. Despite failing at school in the year of the final abuse (aged 9), I even finished top of the class at aged 11 and by God's grace I passed the 11-plus exam and got to Grammar School. I apparently stopped experiencing the pain and depression (which my sister confirmed I'd had), and focussed on learning and God enabled it. I would go so far as to suggest, I was living through the Holy Spirit of Baptism, which gave me Grace and purpose. I remember at the end of the last term at primary school, when others were crying and sad at leaving, I was looking forward to the new adventure!!

However after the final abuse I threw away all toys and dolls, and all 'playing' activities came to an end. In this way I was not able to love God with all I was – because I had lost the playfulness of a child in God's Kingdom. I was like the iceberg with only one tenth visible on the surface.

Secondly: God promises to 'provide for all our needs' (2 Corinthians 9:8, Philippians 4:19) and He did…so I was helped to learn, despite my mother's inability to help me. Through A-level Scripture I was given the opportunity to learn who Jesus Christ was. I pronounced to someone that, 'Jesus Christ was the Son of God; no one's influence can go on for nearly 2000 years without being the Son of God.' And I finished up going into Teacher Training through various failures! 'Though your father and Mother forget you, I will never forget you' (Psalm 27:10). And thus He provided for my spiritual and earthly needs.

Thirdly, after proclaiming faith in Him –God did not leave me to drown in my own wilful ways without help. God had given me great Grace and gifts (I was creative in poetry and in making things) to bring me through the early part of my life, not as an abused child, but as a student, creator and learner. He gave me Love and led and blessed me to serve, for His sake as a teacher.

So in the beauty of His mercy, He had led me after 20 years in Education, (through exhaustion and needing to know humility) back into the church. My life was given back to Christ owning my dependence on His Love for me.

Who sustained me?
What more was necessary? I needed to know the very ground of my being and where my dependance lay, having been totally dependent on my intellect and rational thought. I was already learning greater and greater obedience to the leading of the Holy Spirit, so when I was on retreat at Burford Priory in 1993/4 and felt led to go to the Prayer Room at the top of the Guest House, I went.

I knelt on the prayer stool – wondering but not speaking – when I 'heard', *'I want to give you Mary as your Mother'*. I dared to say, 'But my vicar doesn't believe in Mary'…but my protest fell on lovingly deaf ears.

And I fell into contemplation of this statement.
In front of me to the left was a very large icon of Mary holding Christ.
I tried to imagine Mary holding me. I couldn't.
I tried to imagine Christ holding me. I couldn't.
I tried to imagine the Heavenly Father holding me. I couldn't.

I realised there was a problem. And **dear Reader** if you have experienced bonding problems with your mother, or father, you too may have difficulties 'being a child' receiving love from anyone!!

But God never allows something He has initiated to go unfinished. In my rational mind I was opening up to the reality of what a Mother's love, in purity of heart might mean. After that retreat I met Roman Catholics who 'knew' the Mothering of Mary, and I began to experience it myself as I surrendered more to the mystery of God's healing Presence, being 'held' and fed in Love.

I needed to let go pride and self-protection; and began to intentionally let 'powerlessness' be my strength in Christ – totally trusting in the Father, and the 'wisdom' of Love for the other, while held by God's wisdom and grace.

'Let not your heart be troubled; you believe in God, believe also in Me'. (John 14:1)

Being a child, and totally trusting, even as you grow and make mistakes, means releasing fear of the unknown. How freeing and wonderful that was, for doors opening in my Heart without fear – to see things happening that I did not 'know' but I totally trusted that God knew – and would provide at the right time.

I remember one occasion my Godmother suggesting I produce a community calendar for a particular area of Edinburgh that was going through great upheaval and 'renewal'. I knew the calendar had to be a collaborative activity embracing the elements of this community to help build cohesion and healing. It meant totally trusting in God to lead me one step at a time., never giving in to feelings of being overwhelmed or wanting to control others...but always praying for His Will, harmony and Grace. And thus, even when I had failed to hear – I found a blank space in the calendar – and remembered the prompting I had ignored, so I was finally obedient and indeed His Will could be done! I was blessed with that Grace to know God is God and transcends all for the sake of Love.

Strengthen them in their inner being, that Christ may dwell in their hearts by faith…(Ephesians 3:14-19)

I was pointed to this prayer about 3 years after I had come back into a church – and after praying it consistently for many years, I began to feel the Truth and Wisdom of it...particularly when tackling something like this calendar which had so many people involved. Indeed we need to be strengthened in our inner being through the Holy Spirit as St Paul prays. This strengthening involves many facets of God's means of communication to us and through us: prayer, the Word of God, the practice of 'being in Christ' and knowing His Spirit alive in us. His Word leads us to action, in order for Christ to 'dwell in our hearts by faith'.

Growing in Childlikeness.

Gradually I came to know and love God more, with all that I was, as I followed the Way and passed through more trials. I became more and more 'like a little child' totally dependent on God but open to the rebuke of God to purify me, till I was led to move from Kinston back north.

So now **from October 13ᵗʰ 2021** - God held me in a patient holding of Love, in this flat in Prestonpans, blessing me with gentleness and compassion, and gentle service using gifts He had given me, in humility and grace. But He also blessed me with some elements of the 'toys' etc that I had thrown away as a child. I needed to recognize that 'a bruised reed I will not break' (Isaiah 42:3) applied to me as well....and appreciating God's world was not a sin!!

Dear Reader – see how God enables us to feel our pain, but we have to choose to allow His Grace to move us forward. Our minds cannot work it out – and having learned that – we need to keep hold of that Truth. In humility we need to rest IN our Heart and allow His Grace and Truth to lead us to the next step!!

Wednesday October 13 2021 and the weeks that followed

> Gratitude underpins this being here
> In Loving Arms – blessing and laying balm
> On open wounds – or praise lifting
> And releasing bitter memories.
>
> Day by day the tide washed the shore
> Providing 'play-time' with my coffee –
> To watch the birds and find the regulars –
> And have joy and fun on my door-step!~
>
>
> Thus building me in love for my next task
> On-line, or writing the books, rooting and
> Grounding me in Love, praise and thanksgiving;
> To commit to the work of promised Festal icons.

Dear Reader:

I find it hard to find words – other than His Words, to invite you into these days, weeks and months of sensing myself held in Love. I simply had to be open to receive it, and yet be obedient to the work, in Love that I was still needing to continue, and to grow in the One-ness of being in Christ, obedient to the Father.

> "Abide in Me, and I in you. As the branch cannot bear fruit
> of itself, unless it abides in the vine, neither can you, unless
> you abide in Me.
> "I am the vine, you are the branches. He who abides in Me,
> and I in him, bears much fruit; for without Me you can do
> nothing." John 15:4-5

Open yourself dear soul, to His Love and Presence in obedience to His commandments and direction. In deed He says, *'Follow Me'*. ...and the first step – every day – is to go IN to the Heart in praise and thanksgiving.

2

Rooted and Grounded in Love
Part Two

Love Your Neighbour as yourself ' (Matthew 22:39) - Without worldly certainty: Living for Love ... Praying blessings on 'enemies' and those that have abused. Living in Christ.

13 October 2021

Before I left Kinston I knew my life in Scotland would continue some elements that He had instituted in my life in the latter months in Kinston!

Thus, before the completion of 'setting in order the new flat', in order that I had time for iconography, writing and on-line work for women etc, I was told, *'Do not volunteer'*.   This had been a pattern of behaviour in the past which I had believed to be righteous…. but in truth I had come to recognize the sin of division within me – i.e., when I volunteered to please someone else's mission while denying my own. Thus, God had at times called me a 'prostitute' in doing this, and I had frequently sensed desolation and separation from God as the task drained me of life.

But nevertheless, He made it clear in **December 2021** that as well as writing, which I had been avoiding, I needed to be disciplined about planning and creating and implementing the online courses. And I was prompted to include pastoral visits, the icons I had committed to, and all the ways in prayer or on-line He had enabled me to bear His Love into the world.

Dear Reader, I want you to remember this book is part of a Trilogy, 'He heals the Broken-hearted'. So for me to be given Grace, time and commitment to persevere with these tasks, it means it is part of His calling on my life to be a Witness for and of Him. The students at the Polytechnic back in 1989, who were witnessing God to me, gave me a prophecy, which spoke of the suffering which I would go through, upheld by Him, and that I would become a witness for God. (Isaiah 43) And strangely this prophecy says, 'Because you are honoured and precious in my sight' (Isaiah 43:4).

It is so beyond human worldly comprehension that through our suffering we come to know more of God and His Love and provision and become a witness to God's love. Maybe it is an illustration of *'The stone that the builders rejected has become the chief cornerstone'* (Psalm 118:22).

Comment -I should not have been surprised when even today (Sept 2022) I found myself watching a video and weeping with a mother who had only known a hard-hearted mother who spanked and shouted. Deep in me too, was an unredeemed child who had known little human care or understanding– and all that child had known was 'having to' because there was no choice!! She, I, had had to do everything on my own, with the upholding of my Baptism, but humanly with very limited support, consolation or joy 'Save knowing that I do Your will'. *

But there was LIFE to be owned and lived!!

*This is part of a prayer attributed to St Ignatius Loyola

Teach us, good Lord,

To serve thee as thou deservest;

To give and not to count the cost;

To fight and not to heed the wounds;

To toil and not for seek for rest;

To labour and not to ask for any reward

Save that of knowing that we do thy will.

(St Ignatius Loyola)

I ACCEPT YOUR LIFE in me – and mine in You.

January 27 and 28 2022

God showed me that He had 'imprisoned' me as a child so that I could not go off the rails!! This was His Love. And He made me His obedient child, even though within me was the suffering child who could easily have become rebellious and disobedient but had a broken will! (I remember thinking many years ago – that God was a God of Love; thus, He wanted me to Love, but He didn't Love me!! – here He reveals that His Love was in His tight hold on me!!)

(*I was doing an on-line Spiritual development course and we were asked to reflect on given questions each evening. It was in response to the question about 'the Story we had about ourselves,' that this awareness came to the fore. The following night was about the Identity we had, and now have. God showed me I had been living the cocoon, since I took early retirement and came back into the church, but now had become the Butterfly.)

Today in **September 2022**, I owned the painful humanity of those childhood years and the terrible pain of being unloved, largely ignored, and unwanted by a mother who was unable to love herself or her illegitimate daughter. Alongside that, I was abused and sexually molested by a stepfather. I assume this suffering with Christ, knowing He upheld me through it.

Now (2023) there are no pains associated with this. Sadness and prayer for those who are still suffering, but my pain has gone…. Glory to God.

I give Him all honour for the service He has enabled through turning my pain to prayer for others who are suffering; and the fear overcome in Him.

Dear Reader, only last night in a service in Holy Week, (April 14th, 2023) I was reminded that in our Baptism we are baptized into Christ's Death – and work towards Resurrection. And because of this, as the Father once said to me, '*As you turn to pray* *for others who are suffering the same, it redeems through the Holy Spirit and strengthens others to face their pain.'*

Yet those who suffered, are bound, in their suffering to Him who died that they may live. This is their grounding and rooting in Love when they are willing to receive it. Once we own it, we are free in Christ to be a witness to God's Love and the salvation hidden in Christ.

Overcoming Death for and in Christ

So let us begin with owning our Truth as women of God, whom Christ told, 'Do not weep for Me; weep for yourselves' (Luke 23:28).

Truly it is 'in Christ' that we can face and allow the Healing Grace of the Holy Spirit to bring 'all that is in the dark to the Light'. And believe me dear souls, God can bring the dark to the Light without any effort on your part, or even prayer counsellors or priests!! I was once aware of a darkness in my soul when I was serving and living in Switzerland. I thought I might need to make an appointment with some evangelical pastors I had met during Christian Unity week, but no!

I was on my way to see my Spiritual Father at the Abbey of St Maurice. But I needed to go to the lavatory and was passing a public toilet in the town. I took advantage of the opportunity, but there was graffiti on the wall of the cubicle I entered. My immediate reaction was to run out or at least ignore it, but I sensed I must read it. It was foul, but the Spirit prompted me to forgive and bless the person who wrote it! Wow! I did, and I was immediately set free from the burden I had been carrying in the dark - praying blessings on 'enemies' and those that have abused. Living for Christ. Amen.

This wasn't the first time God had acted 'freely' without any intermediary, to bring me liberation of some darkness risen from the depths that had been clinging to my soul and spirit. But I did need willingness and obedience to His Spirit.

'In God alone I put my trust' – I guess in the end this means releasing all 'material and worldly possessions' and work, in order to enter into Eternity and face all darkness.

I have had to acknowledge the difference between release from false gods and living in denial. As a child I was carried by God in a loveless situation. I came to recognize very early, as a baby when I was ill, and my mother depressed before and after my birth, that I could not expect my mother to carry any burden for me. By God's Spirit I learned to carry my own pain without expectations. This left me without the 'normal' dependence on my mother, and from a human angle, psychologically disabled to love others. But I didn't know I lived in denial, repression and dissociation!! God prepared the way to bring this to the Light…. In the first place I learned these psychological truths towards others, through teaching, in loving and caring for pupils. But this was in the particular relationship of teacher and pupil.

After He had brought me back into the Church, I went on a day retreat called 'What do you want me to do for You?'. I naturally assumed this was the question that I was asking of God!! But the man leading the retreat turned it round. 'What did I want God to do for me?"

He suggested we choose where we wanted to go and consider this in prayer for 30 minutes or so. I wanted to go outside and chose to walk down a path leading away from the building and people. Oh dear! A gate -a shut gate! I turned round and saw all the people on the field. My heart sank. Into my heart came the words, '*These are My people. I would like you to love them*'!

He really had a point!! But could I do it on my own?
Dear Reader – We cannot bring about major changes on our own – but we can turn awareness of our need to prayer to ask God. I was so fixed in 'I have to do this' at that time – I didn't consciously realise God was answering the question we had been

set!!

I simply didn't know how to love others. But with time and the help of the prayers of the Theotokos, change came through obedience to what was being asked of me.

I moved to the Roman Catholic Church as I realised, they did Morning Prayers together (I had been doing them alone) and they had Mass afterwards. The Lord had given me a hunger for the Eucharist from the start at the Anglican Church and taught me that this brought unity and harmony to the Body of Christ – the Church. Soon after joining the early morning parishioners in the Roman Catholic Church, I started 'Catechism' with E – but was also needing to follow up the Anglican Priest's discernment that I go to L'Abri Community in Switzerland for a period. This had been reinforced by one of the monks from Burford monastery discerning that I needed community.

My time in L'Abri gave me opportunity to learn the discipline and joy of harmony, living a monastic-like life. The boundaries and expectations were very clear and for me a delight. Study for half a day, and working for the community the other half, and sharing what you were studying. I had been warned by the Spirit before I left England that I would be living for St Theresa's 'little way of Jesus'. And so it was.

I learned humility in the kitchen, chores needing to be totally obedient to the 'Worker' in charge or needing to humble myself before God (on laundry duty) when I was grumbling about having to 'sort white socks' with a PhD!! The Spirit asked me if I could do it? 'NO,' I had to admit.' *'Then you'd better ask for Grace'*- came the reply! I could still tell you what He taught me about the variations of weave, colour etc on white socks.

I came to appreciate the 'family' interactions with my tutor and his family at breakfasts and on a Sunday tea-time. Yet I needed to learn to hold this joy lightly and 'In God alone I put my trust.' A fellow tutee asked me to swap with his short term visitor who had been put on the breakfast list of another member of staff. I knew I must say 'Yes', but as I grumbled my way down the hill feeling like a 5 year old whose favourite 'thing' had been taken from her – God enabled me to see the sky – totally cloudless except for a tiny cloud over a small plateau on the mountain opposite. I told God He'd forgotten a cloud. *'No my daughter, I left it for you to make you smile.'* And that enabled me to bring my hurting heart to Him and acknowledge it was His kindness to this 'stranger' and it was what He wanted me to do. In the re-connection was immediate release – and I grew in Grace to accept the blessings, and the crosses, of love, with trust in Him.

This period of time in L'Abri gave me so many experiences of the cross. The founder of L'Abri, Francis Schaeffer, was an 'Evangelical' who gave his life, with his wife and family to LIVE for God. Although Francis had died some years before, and his wife was back in USA, the community still never advertised themselves, but prayed every Monday for their needs and those God would send. They helped me see God's work in the Arts, and while there (we had to take a picnic and go out every Thursday) I took people in my car to many different art galleries. I learned so much in this place about humility before God's provision and being more fully human.

Indeed, God asked me to love my neighbours. And He has accomplished it. In Christ is neither male nor female (Galatians 3:28). In Christ, as Children of God, we surrender to God the Father, always willing to ask for His Grace and purpose to prevail. And we will frequently need to say, 'Lord Your will be done,' when something we would have liked to continue, is stopped by others. So be it, and we turn to the Father.

And now in Scotland – still Owning Pain?

God, having emptied me and purified my heart, was inviting me to focus on His Will and purpose in this flat – 'the Retreat of St Chad' with all the rooms dedicated to Celtic Saints but with no daily interaction with other people. I needed to re-focus on what the solitariness was bringing to the Light - no other people making my way – except the responses to those on line – was I running away from anything?

December 30 2021

'Most is unpacked and being used. Today praying about the anger/sadness/powerlessness I was feeling re men's sense of 'right' to dominate and project their 'stuff' on to women who in meekness- accept. Where was God and the Holy Spirit in this?

(Dear Reader – please note how we as women, also 'project our stuff' onto men. I needed to own these feelings….and see how the 'maleness' in me was stopping hidden life.)

'And I stand in You Lord: aware/sad/suffering but I listen to Your Spirit to seek Your Way/Will and I see that I have been reluctant to write because I can't grasp a 'shape' or 'a plan' and stick to it. …abortion happens all the time.

Dear Reader – I believe this difficulty I was expressing was also connected with the desire to 'have control' over what I was doing, rather than doing what God was asking of me….But I was projecting my lack of activity away from myself. I needed to own this and surrender again to God the Father and the Holy Spirit.

'Oh Lord I forgive my mother and her fear that I was to be born. –
I ask Your forgiveness for my collusion with fear about being seen and heard –
even in Your Voice and Love and Truth.

'I see now through your Spirit that a baby is not known until it arrives.
But the mother needs to accept the baby is to be born – and accept the timing and the pain of the birth. AMEN. I accept what is to be born and I will start WRITING a novel /autobiography…..without trying to control by putting it into a 'box'.

Child, alongside this you will PLAN your work re courses and amend dates for the 'Building Blocks of Faith' Course on Master Mind, and website. Advertise on all pages – and continue to build the Broken Hearts course....
-the 'Out of the Depths I have Cried to You' course, Course no 4.
And your icon work...for Kinston.
Allow Me to bear the burdens of ALL this work – Praise – give thanks – AND LOVE ME – as I Love and provide for you – My darling bride.

And I listened to the tasks of the day, after surrendering my heart to His heart and purposes. Without seeking to enliven my Heart with Love, Care, faith, hope and trust each day, my mind could remain cold and sterile, (such as I was projecting onto men in the church) but with His Love and purposes I found His will in directions I did not always expect. Indeed, I needed to 'Stir up the Spirit of the people' in me and be a witness to a Loving and Living God.

Comment

I needed to enter more fully into the mystery of being human – totally trusting in God the Father, the obedience of Christ, and provision of the Holy Spirit. Through this, I become an instrument for the Father, and indeed become a bearer of God the Word, in a sacrifice of self-giving to the glory of God. Maybe in this I will re-find the 'love for my neighbour'?

3

Grasping the Length and Breadth of God's Love' Part One:

Embracing Love for All, for love of God.

I once wrote an essay for the Diploma in Orthodox Studies which asked the Question: 'Who is Christ?'

It was set in the context of St Paul's statement about *'In Christ is neither Greek nor Jew, slave nor free, male nor female, for you are all one in Christ Jesus.'* (Gal. 3:28) In other words, neither the colour of your skin, the culture where you live, nor the philosophy nor 'faith' with which you live, nor your gender, make any difference to being 'in Christ'. The ten Commandments and being obedient to the Life of the Holy Spirit and instructions of God the Father, even unto death, make you alive in Christ – and that Life is accessible in your Heart.

And by God's Grace, long before I came back into the church, I had not only proclaimed Christ as the Son of God, after studying A level Scripture, but following teacher training and becoming a teacher, I sent for and lived with Quaker precepts:

> 1) that there is that of God in all people, and therefore love all.
> 2) serve (in teaching) for love of God, and
> 3) be 'moderate' in all facets of life.

In all my years living according to these precepts I sought obedience and service for Christ's sake, following on from an earlier promise to serve Him. And most of these years I lived with His grace upholding me, I simply believed that I could, and should, persevere in faith in all things…despite exhaustion, and unknowingly, living outside God's commandments for my human life.

I had become an acting Head of 'Inservice-Education for Teachers' Department in a Polytechnic, and following the infidelity and lies of my husband, which led me to leave him; I had been living with a man who had helped me complete my PhD. He supported me with my academic life and enabled me to get a job when my strength was rock-bottom. But ultimately, he did not want to marry me, and I found myself presented with a decision for Christ. In moving out from the conjugal bed, I was led to give my life to Christ in a church.

There are people in the traditional churches who unfortunately dismiss this very act of conscious surrender as something associated with 'evangelicals'….as if this is false and self-negating. God's Love is never false. And God will reach out to His wandering children, in whatever way He can to rescue them from drowning. He'd done it for me when I had actually been drowning, and now He did it for me Spiritually when I was drowning in lovelessness.

The most important things I needed to learn when I was brought back into the church, were my own human frailty and the significance of prayer and the Sacraments. I had taken early retirement by now and I used my time in Bible Study and prayer. I soaked up all the prayer ministry I was able to access. But God taught me that to live for Christ was to serve, in His Grace. And I did that in the Anglican Church, then the Roman Catholic Church, then in Switzerland, and finally led to Scotland under the wing of St Columba.

But how could I continue, without knowing the depth of Christ's love on the Cross? To paraphrase St Paul, 'Who is it that ascended but He who has descended?' (Eph.4:9) So I remember clearly being led to give up seeking and asking for the 'gifts of the Spirit' of Christ and start knocking, seeking and asking to follow St Paul's instruction to seek the Fruit of the Spirit, principally, the 'greater gift' – 'LOVE' (1 Corinthians 13:13).

Seeking to Live for Love

This was particularly significant at a time of great trial and temptation when all my ordered thinking and expectations had been thrown into disarray! I needed to know that ONLY in the power of the Holy Spirit and for God's purposes could I come to live by the FRUITS of the Spirit as Christ did.

This really led me inward and to increasing prayer, to remain conscious not only of what I was doing or saying, but also to open up to the 'other', and to remain open to the Work of the Father at any instant. I was being led into the Dark Night of the Soul, though I only partially understood it.

During this time I released all expectations of God acting on my behalf as a human being, because I had shifted my Spiritual focus. I refused to judge or condemn the behaviour of others or to make childish demands if things were not going 'my way'. On the contrary I grew in awareness that I was to act for Him on His behalf!! He was fulfilling the second part of a prophecy He gave me through students praying for me when He first called me back to the Church. In Isaiah 43 He outlines the trials and suffering that His 'chosen ones' will go through …but goes on to say '..*And you are my witnesses.*'

But He provided for my needs particularly when I had no real spiritual support –every morning in 2018, '19, 20 and most of 21, He would give me, through the Holy Spirit, an understanding or way to behave to guide and carry me through the day.

This was what was recorded **Tuesday February 5th, 2019:**

We will persevere today with icons long promised. We will look to the Father to provide for all needs – material and Spiritual. We will praise.

Child – I know your losses and your emptiness – in your weakness is My Strength.
Be patient and strong to praise – to love – to intercede – to bless – here is your Strength, your Joy – in Me – in My heart of confidence in the Father. I love, forebear, bless and serve in obedience and love for all – yes and forebear all misgivings and unbelief of others – which kills unity and feels like death. Forgive them but keep close to Me and intercede to the Father, 'Father forgive them they know not what they do'.
'Joy', My precious lamb, is hidden in Me. Ask for wisdom as you have – and ask for joy that you rest in My Joy in all you do.
Forgive child those who have crushed you and denied your grace and love, and wanted to destroy your Joy.
PS (later that day) Joy is outward only in Spirit – Joy lifts the other – without words…and protects your soul as you become One with Me… "Enter into the Joy of the Lord".

Following the way of the Cross and doing on-line work

So following a listening time in **December, 2021** I accepted that I had to write for the Lord, *'Tell others what I have done'* and also accept the discipline of continuing with the on-line courses.

When I focused on the 'continuation', I saw precisely what I needed to do. Monthly follow-up Zoom meetings encouraging dear souls to allow Christ to lead them into Light out of darkness, and to continually turn to the Lord in prayer. These were monthly meetings called 'Following the Way'; and new courses were developed: 'He Heals the Broken-hearted' and 'Hearth, Home and Courage'.

I sensed that I should not judge whether they were a 'success' or not but simply seek to be obedient and listen to what the Holy Spirit was enabling in and through me. I became more aware indeed of the extent of Christ's love for the broken and lost, as I surrendered my disappointment, for His Grace and Mercy.

Alongside the courses **in January 2022**

As already mentioned, I had been led to an online 5-day course about the Inner Challenges we face. This was more about inner purification than teaching on-line practices… and as before I was led to reflect on deep questions – which the Holy Spirit answered. I was led to see that for the last 30 years God had kept me as a cocoon, since I had had no external 'life' after He had called me out from overt teaching and service in education. Indeed, all the work He had done in me was internal!! On the penultimate evening of this January course, the question we were asked to reflect on within ourselves, was about our 'Identity'. The Holy Spirit revealed He was setting me free as a Butterfly!!

This was truly life giving. I really felt the Holy Spirit giving me wings, in the Spirit, with joy in Christ, but on the other hand it was a humble 'role' in fertilising flowers and being beautiful in God's Kingdom!! I was told through the Holy Spirit, that I should start a women's prayer group and pray for the world.
So with the collaboration of another Orthodox Christian, I set up the 'World Wide Women's Wave of Prayer'. I pray every Monday at midday, from a Facebook page called 'Women at Prayer; Living for the Kingdom', using Zoom as a meeting platform.

We are now, **March 2023**, in our second year of Prayer meetings. I only know that every week I encourage those who watch to persevere in faith and love, to overcome a specific stumbling block or embrace deeper faith, hope and trust to build themselves and others in Christ, as led and inspired by the Spirit. We pray for the whole world to grow in openness to the Will of God and the Life of the Holy Spirit.
We are seeking indeed to live the 'length and breadth of Christ's Love' in obedience to Christ's obedience to the Father.

4

Living the Height and Depth of Christ's Love-

'Father forgive me I knew not what I did'.

Your will, not mine be done – even unto death

Living for God's commandments are only easy if we are built in faith and trust. Letting go- and Letting God - trusting in the Father's Heart and the truth of what St Paul says, 'in God we live and move and have our being' (Acts 17:28) need to be 'grown into'!

Yet dear Reader, we must remember that our humanity is flawed. But God never abandons His children. Let me back-track to illustrate God's love and mercy.

I loved my work for God in education... that is to say, I loved all those I was given to serve and bless from the youngest to the serving teachers, or mature students. I loved the Grace God gave me to understand knowledge of all forms, and to enable learners whatever their 'level' of need.

And when I followed the Way to give three years to do a PhD, I took all my questions from experience with me. I was asking about the system's assumptions of children's understanding, capabilities, and the need for greater understanding of the schooling process and its effect on learners, and their right and opportunity to 'know' and question.

In the process of the research, I needed to make sense of what I was seeing and hearing, as children from 4 to 16 were living through the schooling process. I wept at some of the misunderstandings I saw within schools and in teachers, and the 'death' of the spirit and soul for some children because of the assumptions and false beliefs that silenced the willing hearts and spirits.

But the work and life for the PhD coincided with the infidelity of my husband. I could have accepted him acknowledging that he had fallen in love with someone, and it was over, but when he denied it, I believed him. Then he told me a week later, on Christmas Eve, he had loved someone. We had people staying for Christmas... the sense of betrayal brought to an end at that time every willing trust and commitment.

I went downstairs from our bedroom to the backroom, and I clearly remember the sense of burning in my flesh – like fireworks going off all over, as I sat with the sense of betrayal of my trust and love. I had no understanding of prayer life at that time - I remember awareness of the coldness of my heart, and that I was separated from it and no longer heard Him in my heart. It took me back to the experience of betrayal of my trust by my stepfather and the unwholesome degradation of my soul.

In 2017 when I was going through a dark time in service, the Holy Spirit spoke to me about this original time of betrayal:

"Once – in God – I turned My back on you to allow the degradation of your soul. Accept that degradation like a precious gift – like an honoured guest in the tomb of Christ. Be conscious only of My Presence with you – and I will raise you from death.'

Thus, back at that time of 'degradation' as I continued to seek integrity, I followed the path the PhD led me on. I moved into teacher education, getting a lecturer position in Bristol separated from my husband and son, but supported by a man who had helped me during my PhD. He supported me to find new work.

How do I make sense of the next few years- living and working in and near Bristol? The economia of God's mercy is beyond comprehension. I was still, in my soul, seeking integrity; but looked at from God's perfection, I was a sinner and adulterer. Yet at that stage I never felt accused because I did not know the law. The man who had helped me became my 'partner' when he had retired, and his divorce was complete. It was through his insistence that God led us to a house that put me in the right place for God to lead me back into the church!!

The weekend before I was going to put in an offer for a house on my own, J insisted on phoning to see if the other house had sold. The agent rang back to say it was. But 10 minutes later the owners rang to say we could have it if we were willing to pay the full price. They had the report for us to see if we wanted to go and see it.

The rest is history and we moved into that house, near practising Christians, and in the next village to the Church where I would be brought back to life in the Church in Faith and Love.

Meanwhile I was experiencing support for my work, and the gradual completion of my task of getting the new structures and courses written and approved for the Inservice- Education for practicing Teachers. Once the new structure was in place and proper support staff and offices set up, I did not apply for the permanent role of Head of Department but asked to be moved sideways to a Student Support role.

Even here God was for me, as they only allocated 3 hours a week for this, and I was given many hours of teaching practice supervision. Previously I enjoyed working with and supporting students and their teachers, but now I had no inner resources to give and care, because I had no love upholding me. J had told me he did not want to marry me, and I realised I could not maintain this situation. This, and my exhaustion in facing the trauma of my childhood revealed through an In-service Course for teachers on 'Recognising signs of Child Abuse' led to despair and no hope. I was truly facing the depths of God's love.

Facing the Depths

When I needed to face my inability to work and maintain 'self-control' in the face of difficult, defensive teachers– and my 'not coping' - I was crying on my bed. This is the mercy of God because I did not consciously know how to pray. My tears were my prayers.

Human resources were withdrawn, but 'He' stepped in. I have told the story elsewhere of God calling my name in 1989/90, and the awareness that deep IN me something was comforted and strengthened. And over the next few weeks, I was given courage to see things happening for my good and wanted to Thank this 'Thing'.

Dear Lord, forgive me I could not even acknowledge you as God, till the students You instructed, started witnessing to me at the Polytechnic and giving me the Prophecies You gave them to give me. Thus began my renewal in the Spirit, but also the conscious salvation of my soul and the renewal of my mind.

But NOW here I was in **2021/22** in this flat by the sea - away from the serving triggered by structures and organisations….and daily facing self-doubt… and daily lifted beyond the lies, to the Truth that God has built in me over the last 30 plus years. I had willingly surrendered my pride and self-sufficiency over the last 10 years – but I was still tempted by deep losses that were still locked in my body and soul.

Dearest Reader – you too may think 'How long oh Lord?- ~How Long?

And I too – here in this beautiful situation, a witness to God's love for me, still going through inner trials to bring all that was in the dark to the light. But God does not abandon you, listen to this –

Thursday 28 October 2021

After I had honoured God for the Grace He gave me to make the two bedroomed flat habitable and functional…. I was aware of a rebellion and wanting something to 'satisfy my soul'…. wanting to turn away from the 'anguish of the cross in my heart'. …

'I sensed I must write this pain/shame/self-hatred at being a woman and unseen and unheard.'

The Cross bears My Name
But I AM is still denied
The Resurrection brought Me home
Yet I AM still denied.
Our Oneness My child
Is in your surrender
To My Will alive in you –
Transforming all losses
To fruitfulness and praise.
I AM setting you free
~From all shame or blame
Relating to past service.
Forgive, bless and intercede
You will be freed
From all double-mindedness-
The devil works even through all
Who do not receive MY Grace
To Love, perceive and bless.

Papa – deliver me from
The darkness that crushes
My will for Good, for Grace.

'This is an old wound child –
Claim your life back from
The curse of abortion –
'Jesus Christ is the Overcoming One' –

Come Lord Jesus into this embryo
And bless me with love
For Your Life in me.
I forgive my mother and father
And all those who have tried
To crush and destroy
My Life and Soul.

The Holy Spirit then spoke directing me to the words of Isaiah 1:6 (which follows a lament for Israel's lack of love and trust in God.)

V6 From the feet all the way to the head, there is no soundness in them, only wounds and bruises and festering sores. They have not been closed or bandaged, or soothed with ointment....

V7 Your land is desolate; your cities are burned with fire. Strangers take over your land in your presence and it is made desolate, overthrown by foreign people.

V8 So the daughter of Zion is forsaken, like a tent in a vineyard, like a hut in a garden of cucumbers, like a besieged city.

V9 Unless the Lord of hosts had left us a seed, we would have become like Sodom and been made like Gomorrah.

> After I had agreed that this was true, He said,
> *"I will make you a fisher of men"*
> *Without blame or shame and in My Love,*
> *Compassion and Purity of Heart.*
> *Nothing will separate you from the Love and Word of God.*

So along with writing the courses and providing on-line 'Following the Way' continuation to encourage faith Living, I was also aware of the need to continue writing a book.

Writing without 'Listening' –

I had had the idea of writing a novel for some time, so I thought that was what I was to do. But in fact, I started writing up previous hand-written books of phases of my life. I started typing them up and added some facets involving the reader in seeing heroine/hero, 'the story' and how the life challenges affected the heroine at different stages and overcoming them. I ignored some misgivings in my soul and had nearly completed this and had sent sections out to various readers for comments.

It was while one of these, a priest-hermit, was discussing it with a fellow hermit, who had been an editor in earlier life, that the Lord interrupted their conversation. He said this book was more to be left for my grandchildren...but now He wanted something more specifically focussed on His work. Fr Stephen got in touch with me and told me of this 'conversation' – which I accepted because I knew I had not followed through on the previous writing He had led me to do in the Parish.

So I dug out the 'listening to the pain' writing and I started to seriously aim towards making it a book. After one particular session, with the Holy Spirit, I was called to sit down to listening prayer.

I heard *'This is to be a Trilogy called, 'He Heals the Broken Hearted.'*
The First: 'Treasures of Darkness: Facing the Pain and Finding the Light.'
The Second: 'Your Will Be Done: Beyond Powerlessness Fear – Life Revealed in Love.'
And the Third: 'Children of God: Conformed to the Life-Giving Cross in Joy and Hope in Eternal Life.'

I finally focussed on the realities of publishing a book and asked for information and help at church and on-line. So with guidance for the process for Book One and an on-line course on self-publishing on Amazon– I got readers, and an editor – and a formatter from Church – with a recommendation from a Bishop... ... This writing persevered as I knew the 'emptiness' within my soul, but alongside His provision in Love.

But I am going ahead of myself. All those first 6 months of my time in the flat were a building of my Life in Christ, as it was, but a preparation of what was to come. I had an awareness of God telling me while still in Kinston, that I would suffer again when I moved- with an intuitive sense of April '22 being a turning point. I sought to press on, while living day by day with intermittent human support – but always aware of St Chad and my protecting saints St Seraphim and St Silouan. Glory to God.

So, my days were held in God's love: the on-going needs of the on-line work; the commitment to writing up the First Book*; appreciation of the sea and the provision of a permanent 'bird-hide'; and gradually getting re-familiar with the Parish in Edinburgh. I trusted God and regular confession to deal with my sense of alienation. Because of the cost of petrol, I tended to only go into Edinburgh on Sundays when I fulfilled my pastoral visits after church.

Iconography

An important element of the days prior to April 2022 was the work on the two icons for Kinston Parish. Given their subjects they tied in with the work within me. While persevering with the Crucifixion – the suffering of Our Lord and the anguish of Mary and St John dwelt in my heart and soul – and complemented my own anguish. Yet I knew I was doing God's Will' and was forgiving all.

It was a joy to start the Resurrection – with bright colours and the Joy of Salvation being our Promise. Glory to God.

I could see I was going to be ready to deliver the icons to Kinston before Easter, so I made arrangements to stay with A at her house in Stafford.

Saturday 9 April 2022

Travelled after TMES teaching on line to stay with A in Stafford.

Sunday 10 April

I delivered the two icons to Kinston Church – then went with A to see the families we had shared life with when I had worked in the Parish. A joy to see people at church.

Drove home safely.

Book Focus

From then till August, I was building up the commitment to publishing Book 1. I was following advice of others who had done this before and had made a course. I did eventually set up a Facebook Page for the Trilogy; after needing to write succinct 'accounts of the book' from various angles. I realized how alien it was to me to write almost objectively about this 'work of God' at the same time as seeking to appeal to a reader who might find the book helpful. Glory to God I did write something, (many times) for the headings they suggested, and I began to understand why this clarity of thought was essential to communication. It helped me too.

But I get ahead of events. On **August 6ᵗʰ 2022,** the Feast Day of The Transfiguration, I was on my way to pick up RA and P to take them to Liturgy. I was slightly later than I intended and was not praying my way to the car. I suddenly found myself doing a shoulder charge with my right shoulder onto the junction of pavement and wall as I tripped over an uneven paving slab. Oh dear!!

I prayed my way 'still' and tried to move. I realised I had no power in my right arm to push myself up. In God's mercy, a man walking on the other side of the road, must have seen me fall as he came across the road to help despite the fact that I was by then hidden behind a parked car!! I was still focussed on going to Liturgy so when he got me on my feet, I said I was fine and actually went to the car.

I unlocked it and got into the driver's seat and tried to move my right arm to put the keys in the lock. I could not. After several attempts to reach my arm forward – I discovered I could move my arm forward with my left arm, but still had no power to turn the key! I realized I was not safe to drive, got out, locked up and went back to the flat to ring RA.

C, RA's husband, came on the bus, and rang those who know these things, to find the best place to take me….and gave them my phone number. By the time he arrived, I was on the phone being assessed for the damage, and then we were phoned with an appointment time for Minor Injuries Clinic at the Royal Infirmary in Edinburgh. By 1:30pm I had been X-rayed and assessed …. No broken bones but obvious movement restrictions!! I left with a referral for a 'Torn shoulder-cuff (?)' being sent to the Orthopaedic surgeon. C brought me home with my arm in a sling and painkillers.

10 days later I had a phone call from the surgeon suggesting that to begin with I go for physiotherapy The pain was intense and only with the extra painkillers, which the physiotherapist insisted I get from the doctors, was I able to start doing the movements she recommended!!

I did see the surgeon after a couple of months as the progress was VERY slow and I was afraid that without surgery I would be permanently disabled. I did have the MIR scan which confirmed the condition…but my only option involved a new shoulder because the cuff could not be repaired a second time.

Dear Reader – I guess we always want healing quickly and without pain! That's not what we are promised!! So now March 2023 – I will be having my last physiotherapy session in April. I am taking far fewer painkillers and am gaining some movement via another muscle in the shoulder. For some movements, I still have to lift my arm into position but that is gradually improving. It gets tired quickly and I fail to do anything with 'weights' -at present. I decided against the operation as that would be at least another 3 months of pain and inaction for a doubtful result. Despite my weakness, I can now hang out washing again (ie get my arm to the washing line and fasten a peg in place…not lift the washing up to the line!!) getting my arm up above my shoulder – something I was told was unlikely. And these movements have led to restoration of my icon painting!!

I have learned more humility, patience -and need to accept painkillers and kindness of many people! Indeed, just as with my soul, hidden in Christ in God, there are real changes – and healing beyond expectations! I knew when I damaged my shoulder back in 2014, I was being invited to share in the physical suffering of Christ. Somehow this pain was more extreme, and debilitating, and I had no young people around to provide for my needs on a regular basis.

And yet I was upheld by God the Father and was able to persevere with the writing and on-line work.

It certainly underlined for me that I could not expect protection from evil unless I was praying and really listening for God's will. What was God asking of me?
'Yet I will praise You Lord.'

5

Able to do exceedingly abundantly above all that we ask or think, according to the power that works in us

Trusting, even in emptiness and poverty…and with the Butterfly – praying and offering a different voice to others.

Love God with All you are: Have no false images.
St Paul's definition of 'Love' making Unity in the world
Trusting in the Father –

Deep in my Heart, from the early days of being in the church, I believed in, sought, and prayed for Unity in the church, churches, and in ourselves. Maybe for some time I lived in deafness or denial of all the divisions and the active dismissal of one church by another. But maybe God was holding me in the beauty of His Love and Grace as I sought to live for Him? As I moved from the Anglican to the Roman Catholic and then to the Orthodox Church, I was blessed by people to follow God's calling. I never moved with animosity or judgement in my heart, but only with a sense of obedience to the Way. And loving priests would bless me, and God made it easy as He never allowed anything to 'hold' me in one church or another. Even to the extent that while in the Roman Catholic church in Edinburgh I did preparation to become a Eucharistic Minister. But I was never called for the initiation blessing! I accepted this loss– and shortly afterwards I was led into the Orthodox Church. …

For me, the Way was seamless. I was simply opening my heart door to become more complete in Christ. And still now, I love all facets of God's provision for the Body of Christ, reaching out to different people with different preparedness and gifting. I pray for openness to the leading of God through His Word, the Body of Christ, and the purification of our hearts.

Dear Reader, Let's be honest, there is NO part of the Body where **all** its people are living by the Holy Spirit in Spirit and in Truth, all the time. In fact, St Paul says we all fall short of the Glory of God, (which comes from greater and greater surrender to the Holy Spirit's Life in us) and St John says that *'we lie if we say we do not sin.'* (1 John 1:10)

So, as I came to live and serve in and for the church/es I saw and experienced the divisions –as I grew in Christ and had 'eyes to see'. However I needed to lean on His Love even more and count Christ as my Redeemer –'*And He Himself is the propitiation for our sins, and not for ours only but also for the whole world.*' (1 John 2:2). I was led to embrace the first Commandment – to Love God with all my Heart, Mind and Soul and Strength, above all; and to make no image of God. Unfortunately, this is the danger with the divisions of the church, and our man-made images of what God wants, does, says, etc. in danger of all forms of self-righteousness.

So, despite apparent division, I seek at all times to holding on to Christ's word and keep PRAISING…I trust even in emptiness and poverty that forgiveness, blessing and seeking to live for His Love, will lead to Peace, Patience, Joy, long-suffering. I have needed to let go of all the many false gods that give pleasure, self-satisfaction, vainglory, or spiritual 'self-righteousness.' I live in trust that my nothingness can lean on His Everythingness as my only comfort.…and with the Holy Spirit giving the Butterfly wings – praying and offering a different voice to others. Do I fall? Yes, I do, but if I turn to Him miracles happen!

Able to do exceedingly abundantly above all that we ask or think, according to the power that works in us,'

The title of this chapter has been lived out many times as I've seen His work through me even in very practical ways, when I had nothing to offer in terms of human strength or courage. He responded in one particular day to the need to get my new flat in Craigmillar habitable with the help of students from church. Despite their reluctance to accept my knowledge and understanding of how to lay laminate boards, (I am a woman after all!!) we did get the walls painted, and the living room laminated and then I went on to fulfil other steps in preparing this flat for habitation. I sensed my awareness of the Grace that was carrying me, at a point quite late in the afternoon when more work had to be completed - and this part of the prayer was still being fulfilled. It must be noted that this Grace meant I could make the move to be in an area God wanted me to be – and leave the quiet and beauty of Kintyre. Maybe God was 'preparing the way' for me, knowing my need for encouragement!

Another time I had come back to this now lived in flat, having been across to a friend who had difficulty managing life. I had worked with her to clean and re-create some order and had cooked. I came back to my flat – feeling exhausted and aware of the untidiness and need for cleaning in my own flat. I prayed to the Father, without grumbling, but stating my need and exhaustion – and I came into the flat. The flat was tidied, cleaned, and washing up done etc in less than an hour – without any stress!! Glory to God. I felt as if I had had Mary Poppins visiting!! – in me!!

Now 6th September 2022 – I was being challenged by God to love Him with all I was – and to consider the Word in 1 Kings (chapters 4-6) and prophecy in Revelations 21:3-5. I wrote the following as a blogpost on my Joy of All Who Sorrow website as in invitation to a group:

"**Dearest Reader**, I want to show you the root, and God's purpose of this group.
As you know from previous blogposts and my work over the last 3 years on-line, I am always 'knocking, seeking and asking' (Luke 11:9-10; Matthew 7:7-8), and sharing it with you. This is not to 'show off' but to offer the new perspectives on our lives that God has revealed when I've been in difficult or apparently destructive situations.

'Faith' has burrowed into dark places and brought Light and Resurrection to old deaths bringing me greater integrity. Hope has given perseverance wings to carry me in Loving ways when all seemed dark from a human perspective. And Love has purified my life taking the 'old man' thinking, fears and should and ought's, to enable me to stand in Spirit and in Truth.

I was asking God in my emptiness, where He wanted me to go with all this? and first He led me to a reading (1 Kings:4) about the capturing of the Old Testament Ark of the Covenant (the Promise of God) which was so significant to the Jews. If you remember, the Tabernacle held all the Holy Articles, the Rod of Aaron that Sprouted life, (signifying the Living Priesthood): some of the Manna (food) that the Israelites received each morning when they were in the desert (signifying the Living Word of God that feeds us daily, and the Eucharist); and also the stone with the Ten Commandments, (signifying the Ways of God that we need to follow).

The battle in which the Israelites were defeated by the Philistines led to the capture of the Ark of the Covenant. Initially there was great rejoicing but then the Philistines discovered that the Living God was not going to bless their false idols and life. After many trials the Philistines of Asdod who worshipped an idol called Dagon, decided to pass on the Ark, and the people of Gath welcomed it. They too could not bear the trials they received, and so it passed to the people of Ashkelon, who eventually cried out to the Philistines to take it back to the people of Israel. It was finally returned to the people of Israel with due respect. (1 Kings 4-6)
God proved Himself to be present in this Ark of the Covenant. And for the Jewish people the elements of the Ark gave them their faith which enabled them to stand with many trials over the years, though they too were not always faithful to God.
And that is why Christ came to earth as the New Testament - a Living Tabernacle of all those things included in the Ark - Priest, Living Food and Word, and Fulfiller of the Law in Love.

But I was still knocking, seeking and asking about where I was going with this Word about the tabernacle. And then the following came to me - a Scripture reference.

'Behold I make all things new'. Revelation 21:3-5
….And He said to me, "Write, for these words are true and faithful."

…And He said to me, ….
"He who overcomes shall inherit all things, and I will be his God and
he shall be My son.
(Revelation 21:6-8)

This is God's Word to all of those who believe in Christ and His Love, Saving Grace, and who desire to persevere in Life to Him and with Him. I was so encouraged by this because I had lost sight of the GOAL! I was in effect 'surviving' in Christ because of all the trials! So God is encouraging me, to encourage YOU to re-grasp the Goal which leads to the Kingdom, and Eternal Life.

Does it mean we are either condemned for not being there, or immediately taken up to heaven? No dear ones, even Jesus said, 'Those who **endure** to the end will be saved' (Matthew 10:22). This is encouragement to endure, **with joy, faith, hope and grace in Christ** so we can be living witnesses to Christ - 'come in the flesh'. And we are encouraged to do it together, seeking fellowship with like-minded, God loving - God-living Volunteers who desire and seek the Will of God in all humility and courage. In 2013, God spoke to me when I was feeling despair:

Overcome all darkness – despair,
Fear, shortcoming –by
Holy Trust in the Eternal Grace
Of God the Almighty Father
Through the Incarnation.
This Will always bring Peace,
Love, Joy.
These are not sentiments –
Not human constructs
But statements of Being in God.-
Given in God, by God, for God.
Let Me win my darling daughter.

NB Wherever you are – whatever you do – you will be tempted to despair – to sloth- to lovelessness – to give more of yourself to appease Me…although you have given all in moving here and leaving your dream in beautiful places, simply turn and pray, and ask.

Shortly after the above - I was listening while at the monastery, while holding a question in my heart about 'confidence' and not wanting to crush anyone:

> *Child – dearest one*
> *Gentleness is full of Holy Strength*
> *Without self or worldly power*
> *But full of Grace and Truth.*

Lord come to us and abide in us that we may be Lights in the Darkness.

So here I am with this offering of a members Group for those who truly want to tread onward: sometimes inward, downward, upward, or forward - according to the leading of the Holy Spirit, and God's Life and Love in YOU. …. and your willingness to leave your agenda at the foot of the Cross and go with Christ into your Heart.

But don't be afraid; *'Seek first the Kingdom of God and His Righteousness and all these things shall be added to you.'* (Matthew 6:33)"

I went on to put this post on the Joy Of All Who Sorrow web site – but did not 'publish' it. When set up it would be approached through an email -and the post led to an invitation and link to a private group on the website. I had to tackle more on-line technical difficulties to try to set up a group.

However, at the same time as doing this I was persevering with Book 1 of the Trilogy, 'He heals the Broken Hearted'; and I was seeking to set up an appeal for the Kenyan I supported in prayer,

as he and the rest of the refugees were threatened with eviction.
I felt I was walking in the dark in relation to publishing the first book…but in September had realised that I needed to communicate its potential existence! Thus, I followed advice on the publishing course and set up a Facebook page for the Trilogy and started to collect email addresses of people who were interested in finding out more about it. The Bishop also gave me a recommendation for the book – which became a Forward…with part of it as a recommendation to be included on the Book Cover. All this had to go to the Cover Designer to be put into action to provide for the publishing of the paperback book.

I was also still creating, doing, offering, and running courses during this time in particular one which used the 'poem' that the Holy Spirit had given me many years before for the Craigmillar Calendar, to enable people to start to grasp the nature of 'being' and 'becoming' in everyday life. In using the poem with questions, it enabled people to listen within themselves and discover more of their Inner Being and find their current need of God's love and wisdom to bring the dark to Light.

Dear Reader – Life IS….. and in humility I simply prayed and trusted and allowed the Holy Spirit to carry me with appointments, including a shoulder appointment at the hospital; the on-line work that needed attention; and the need to continue to be open to learning about publishing the book. I was in the last stages of the book and, having found a means of making the Kindle version of the book I was able to set a date over a week ahead for the publication. However, I then needed to accept a delay in the publication of the paperback book as there were minor technical modifications to do on the KDP publishing site! I was in deep water, but Andrew from church helped me on the path and both the paperback and Kindle versions were published ☺

Friday October 28 2022

Book Launch on Zoom. I smile to myself at the courage I was given to simply 'do it'*. I was grateful for the disparate people from all over the world who came in response to the email invitation and an on-line friend co-hosted so she could admit people onto Zoom. After readings from the book, there were questions and comments.

God had indeed worked things in new dimensions of my life and carried me in faith each day.

*__And Dear Reader__, truly NOTHING separates you from the love of God…and when you simply ACCEPT what IS and the work that is to be Loved into being – there is no worry or anxiety. This is why so much is possible and is without pride or vain-glory because I know the work is done through me, but not by me!! And yet there is constant flow and exchange of Love and awareness which means I never feel used or abused, because my will is involved and my desire to love and bless and provide is fuelled through and by His Love. Others may talk of 'energies' which is part of the picture – but Dear Reader, you too may want to Live and Serve in Love, having known the trauma of abuse. Christ was 'Incarnate' – as a human being – and He is alive in us too as we give ourselves to His Life and purposes in us.

6

To know the love of Christ which passes knowledge; that you may be filled with all the fullness of God

Yielding to the Spirit and purposes of God.

In **September 2022** I had been filled with zeal and the Holy Spirit to see how a vision of the New Jerusalem was indeed life-giving and encouraging for Christians. I had created a way to bring Christian women into a context on-line where they could choose for opportunities to meet one to one with me, and with the group for Q and A sessions to engage with living out this Vision of the New Jerusalem. In either they could ask questions, share what God was doing, and the stumbling blocks they need to overcome to Live fully by the Word of God and the Grace of Christ.

But something was stopping me 'launching' this opportunity. Partly this was my uncertainty about charging a monthly subscription to help me maintain the necessary on-line facilities, yet largely an 'unknown' held me back*.

*Dear Reader, Over, this last 18 months, I had needed to grow much more sensitive to the 'voice' of the Holy Spirit, through the Heart of Christ within. He only did what the Father told Him to do, or what He saw the Father doing. In this case with the potential launch of this group and pointing people to the goal posts of our lives, I had two different 'stop' signs. In my uncertainty about charging, I had both human desire to charge for money so I didn't have to worry about all the on-line fees, but this was counter-balanced by such Truths as *'Freely you have received, freely give'*. I handed this all back to God, in the Light of the other 'stop' sign. I simply had no will to go forward with it. The Truth of this was not in question – but maybe the timing to appeal to others was not right. I had learned a lot about timing over the last few years, as I'd needed to wait for His timing to open doors in my heart and mind in order to make a particular step. This was how I perceived this 'Stop'. And now May 2023, I am still holding this in obeyance to find God's will and purpose…but meanwhile the Eternal Truth has been fulfilling its Light in me.

I was also getting towards the completion of Book 1. *
*I wrote this **Dear Reader** as if I had written 'I had cereal for my

breakfast'.... But my editor picked me up on it asking for some Comment. He is right of course. The whole thing is an inordinate act of Grace. And to God be the Glory!! I had learned some time ago through Gestalt Psychology, that to know 'completion' of anything – we need to 'receive' it – own it. So just as we need to own our pain and losses and the trials we are given, and thus we come to know more of ourselves and the Love of God, so we need to 'receive' and 'own' those awesome acts of 'overcoming' through Christ when we have a gift offering to give to God and the world. Glory to God. And this awareness of a shift in me through this near completion of the book, and the New Jerusalem writing, tied in with God moving me within to shift my perspectives.

October 13 2022

As the anniversary of my move from Kinston came and passed, I became aware of a 'shift' of perspective. I saw that God had provided me with a year of self-care – enabling me to complete the icons that I had promised to Kinston and build my writing to new commitment levels as He restored my soul.

Earlier in the year, having been warned by Fr Stephen, and my own conscience, I had refocused my writing on the book I had started in Kinston ... the one facing my pain. I had found out what to do – and did it....simply following the steps laid out by others who had published before!

October 28 2022

As I have previously said we had a book launch on Zoom, and both a Paper back and Kindle version came to be published on Amazon. To some extent I was still living in denial – but I knew this was for God's purposes and in all things, I surrendered to Him, not least as I had no sense of an opening or direction.

'I know the plans I have for you.'

But God had other plans for my life than to stay alone in this flat! Throughout the year I had been back in Edinburgh parish I had been regularly visiting an older friend in Edinburgh. I had realized how alone she was and had wondered if I should offer to become her companion. But I wasn't sure she could accept it – or if I could whole-heartedly offer.

On the Sunday after the Book Launch, as I was praying before I went to church, I heard the Lord say, *'I'm going to give you a new Heart.'* I thanked Him and gave Him my will…but knew the 'action' was in His hands. On the way to church I suddenly had a bitter, angry thought come into my mind. For some time now, I had been responding to all 'enemies' of Christ within, or without, simply with 'blessing.' So, I started blessing this enemy in my mind. After the third or fourth blessing this bitterness within turned into pain. Then I knew that I needed to repent of not turning to God with this pain but trying to handle it myself and find comfort in the world. With the repentance came comfort and surrender to God.

By the time I got to church, I knew He had indeed put a 'new Heart' in me. I simply wanted to surrender wholeheartedly to His Life in the Church once more; He asked me to kiss the Cross instead of kissing His icon. Eventually I saw the large Cross to the left of the Altar area and in trust went to honour Him in His Cross.

'Who do you see?' He asked.
As I sat in the church:
And my heart was filled with
Awareness of those who
Had gone before in total
Trust and obedience –
Bearing His Love and Grace
To honour the Life
That God the Father
Gave, and took away.

I wanted to be with
My Brothers and Sisters,
To be One with them
In Christ - glorifying the Father.
And yet I knew in Truth,
There was no place in
This church building I could physically live.
What did God want of me?
What had I to give?

After Church I went to spend some time with one dear soul I regularly saw on a Sunday, then went to Jean's for her weekly visit. As I pulled up at her house, I was surprised to see KN's, her Power of Attorney, bicycle outside. He never came on a Sunday! Just then he came out and I asked him how Jean was. He explained the current situation: a morning carer had been arranged, but he commented that she was quite depressed. I found myself saying that I had been thinking about offering myself as a living in companion and asked him what he thought. He immediately commented that I would need my own space – and suggested that I ask Jean to see what she thought–we would all pray about it.

When I asked Jean, she was enthusiastic…but I needed to speak to my Spiritual Father which had to wait for his return the following Thursday. In principal he thought it was a good suggestion but recognized that old people can change their mind when facing a reality…so he suggested a trial period to ensure Jean wanted me in the house full-time.

After this post-Vespers meeting, I went to tell Jean who was touched by B R's thoughtful concerns. We agreed I would come for a trial period on **November 9th** bringing my absolute essentials to be able to live upstairs without disturbing her food and organisation in the kitchen.

KN made arrangements for a man with a van to pick up my fridge and essential bedroom storage, iconography materials, and my computer and writing needs, to move me into Jean's first floor spaces. Only minor shifts of Jean's upstairs furniture needed to be made at that stage.

The Bishop had offered to come and bless the house – so after 8 days of living together the house was blessed, Jean confirmed she did want me to stay, and the move was blessed too.

Reflection on Learning 'Obedience'

In the earlier years of my walk in Christ, I had read many of the classic 'Spirituality' books which inspired me to know more of God and to find His Heart, Mind and Will.

I lived in Kintyre in 2008 onwards with a conscious **'Abandonment to Divine Providence'** – a book by Fr Jean-Pierre de Caussade. He counsels us to 'abandon yourself entirely to God by embracing the duties of your station in life'. With wisdom and gentleness, he teaches how to practice complete submission to the will of God in every situation, whether we are beginners or seasoned travellers on the way of perfection. 'True abandonment,' he explains, 'is a trusting, peaceful, and childlike surrender to the guidance of grace.'

So each day at that time, all my 'choices' were surrendered to: what I was told to do by the Spirit; 'what happened'; or the requests made of me. I saw how an interior instruction, (like joining a mutual help community in the town, which I had not known about) led to me providing support for a young family newly transplanted to Campbeltown. Specifically, they needed 'family' support for occasional baby-sitting for their young son and led to me taking them to Christmas Lunch at the Salvation Army joining them to a wider family. And this mutual help community also provided a team of men who came to help move a shed in my garden when I had need.

I gave myself to re-training to give literacy help which led: a) to two women who were also doing the training, asking me to help them start a U3A* group in the town. I gave them a year, acting as Chairman, and left them after giving them training in 'facilitating' others.

(*The University of the Third Age invited retired people to share their expertise and interests with others – we developed both a monthly programme of talks when people got together on a regular basis, and also a selection of interest groups –classical music, and walking come to mind.)

But also, b) after seeing my CV, the Local Adult Education officer enrolled me as a tutor for various community projects.

My service for God in the Community began to be full-time! Then, the involvement in a Churches Together group for helping the homeless when being re-housed, grew with the size of the task. We needed to become an 'official charity' as we were handling money! Truly the Lord promises to supply all our needs! I was made Treasurer, and somehow with the support of the Salvation Army Treasurer, I was enabled to do what was needed…without any sense of being gifted in that area!!

Following the Salvation Army Major's request to me to take the course for qualification in Food Hygiene I received a constant, and regular, role in the Salvation Army work with the homeless, after-service hospitality and even the special meals laid on at Christmas. I had great respect for the Major, who was tireless in her commitment, despite much physical pain. My Orthodox Spiritual Father had blessed this work and used to say that the Salvation Army had very sound dogma. I was very blessed by her honesty with me and the gentle challenges she laid at my feet when she saw some unhealed hurt in action. She also valued my prayers, and my willingness to accept her kind and pure challenges. It was her gentle comment that I was always late for church, that led to my recognition of a half-heartedness and unwillingness to totally commit. And God was leading me to face this hidden heart, firstly through reading.

The Cloud of Unknowing

Another book that I had read which began to have new significance, was the 'Cloud of Unknowing'. 'The Cloud of Unknowing' is an anonymous work of Christian mysticism written in Middle English in the latter half of the 14th century. The text is a spiritual guide on contemplative prayer. Through Surrender to Providence the human spirit is opened up to see God at work as described above, and at the same time a growing awareness of, and surrender to, 'Unknowing'. Truly I could no longer judge what was happening. I was being drawn into more stillness, on one hand, but God was shaking all assumptions on the other!

House Blessing and More Mystery

When I moved to Campbeltown I had invited the priests from the church in Edinburgh to come and give the house a blessing. After a failed attempt on his own, the young priest brought my Spiritual Father, and they stayed the night and blessed the house. I had invited all the ministers, priests, and clergy of Campbeltown churches to the blessing. Most came, and all were invited to share the food afterwards, but only the Roman Catholic priest and the Roman Catholic Hermits stayed. What a blessed evening: at the end of which my Spiritual Father blessed me to share Spiritual support with the hermits – specifically with Fr Stephen, the priest/monk.

I add this because after this visit the hermits had a revelation that they were to give to me, for the Orthodox Church, the church on an island they had hoped to make into a monastery.

I was truly in a Cloud of Unknowing and only silence and Prayer was to provide a way, but I was unable to respond wholeheartedly at that time. So, I responded in action.

Thus, even though while still in Campbeltown I had sensed the call to become like a recluse and write... my rational mind 'didn't know' who St Theophan the Recluse was – or what I was to write!! So I followed the invitation to the Island Church to prepare the way – as I thought.... but the call to write came to fruition by God's Providential care and His Grace 2 years later and led to 'Treasures of Darkness: Facing the Pain and Finding the Light,' the first of the Trilogy of books.

Listening, Prayer and Service – facing the Dark-night of the Soul

The time of listening and surrender in Wales (2012-2013) led to greater purification of what had been hidden in the dark, and thus to more committed service. So in the following 10 years from 2013 to 2023; the Holy Spirit has worked in my soul and spirit to purify and cleanse all my history even further as I was challenged to serve in Love. 'Your Will Be Done: Beyond Powerlessness Fear – life Revealed in Love' tells the story of the service 2014-2021.

- I surrender daily to where I am, which meant I needed to face not simply my own sin rising to the surface, but the effect of the sins of 'fathers and mother'. It was a time for absolute integrity of body and soul, heart and mind. No more denial or repression. I needed to own, experience, and forgive, or 'bless your enemies' for every trial I had suffered, and every death I had allowed to remain unmourned, or unredeemed. As Jesus says: 'Not one jot or tittle will be left unturned'. And it is His Spirit and Word (with our Yes) that continues the work.

So, I lived daily with 'unknowing' yet knowing I was in God's hands and Love. "Nothing can separate us from the Love of God'.

And living in silence and prayer became the norm – but without 'fear'. * I grew in Grace to depend on the Jesus prayer, and the descent to the Heart. There was always gentleness and obedience in the Holy Spirit – and encouragement for my human heart, when I was tempted to despair through wanting to be loved, or to see the way forward.

*I am frequently reminded, when I am tempted to be 'macho' in my choices, the time in Campbeltown when my central heating broke down, and at that time I had no hot-water bottle. I prayed and asked the Lord for more Grace to go to bed. Suddenly I saw my dog (who was not allowed on the bed except on her blanket at the foot of the bed in the morning) jump on top of the bed to lie where my body would go. It was so clearly an 'act of God' I simply prepared for bed – and as soon I was ready to get in, she jumped down and went into her own bed. She did this every night while I had no Central heating… and whenever it was cold and inhospitable. Clearly, I was not called to excessive asceticism!!

What is so wonderful is that this descent to the Heart with all the essential healing, repentance, and surrender, led to greater Trust, and acceptance of my human weakness. Gradually the self-hatred was purified through growing understanding of what it is to be human, called to Divinity through the Holy Spirit.

The Holy Spirit made it clear to me that no-one (all made in the Image of God) can carry the loss of being despised and rejected, without suffering harm to their soul – Christ suffered a 'broken-heart' on the Cross. Only through the Father's Love and healing can this damage to the soul, body and mind be resurrected and restored to Grace. And the two simple prayers that I clung to like drift wood in a stormy sea, 'Lord I believe, help Thou my unbelief', and 'Lord I am willing to be willing to be willing – to do your will..' expressed my weakness and need for His Love and work. I trusted every time that He would bear the burden and bring new life and healing when I received His Body and Blood in the Eucharist. According to His Word, while I persevered with praising, praying and serving, He gave me more of His Life.

What is the effect on the soul? Total trust in God the Father, and desire to praise, give thanks and intercede as He leads. The Commandments and the Beatitudes become ALIVE in Love and the Holy Spirit. And the Love makes every trial a Joy in knowing more of Christ. God indeed is Love – and wants to bring us to His Purity of Heart and Purpose, so we become vessels of Grace, Truth, and Witness to His Love.

And NOW November 2022, I was brought to a new dimension of surrender in obedience to His Love alive in me.

7

More than you can ask or conceive - Holy Emptiness

Writing AND moving .– St Paul's statement 'In Christ is neither
male nor female..'

Thursday 17 November, 2022

B R came to bless Jean's house, and prayed for me to permanently
move to be with Jean as her companion.

Friday 18 November, 2022

I gave in my notice for my flat, with Touchstone Housing Association.

Somehow, I was given grace to marry together Jean's needs for a companion, on-going work with Book 2, on-line commitments, and the necessity to make arrangements to move.

My immediate need re Jean was to 'learn' her routines and needs such as being a provider of mid-morning coffee, lunch, afternoon tea and 'supper'. These had particular times, yet flexibility was often necessary both from her state, sleep etc, or a commitment I had. We were needing to work together, and I realised that in Love I needed to communicate the difficulty I had when she ordered me to do things. As a result, she began to ask rather than demand, and her whole demeanour and our relationship grew in Grace and Love, even tenderness.

I learned to fit things round her needs yet encouraged her to still make her own coffee or tea if I could not get back in time. Her lunches, which were good quality frozen meals, were cooked in the micro-wave – and for the first few weeks she could still do this for herself when it was necessary, if I had told her she needed to do it.

She ate her main meal at midday, when I ate my celery and humous snack with her. In the evening I gave her supper of sandwich and cake, often with some fruit, while I ate my meal.

Conversation was not easy as she had had a minor stroke some months before, so her articulation was not always clear. This made it hard for loving members of her brother's family to have a conversation with her over the phone. I learned to use the 'listen with the Heart' technique which I had had to learn when in Switzerland and France – in order to allow the Holy Spirit to give me understanding of French talks or sermons I needed to listen to.

I was tired at the end of each day and was normally in bed soon after 9pm, which had been my pattern of rising early, and retiring early for a long time. But I prepared the way for Jean to retire putting on the lobby and bedroom lights, closing her bedroom curtains and opening her bed, and putting out her night-time tablets in the kitchen. Although the Power of Attorney was trying to get a night carer to put her to bed – it never happened and as Jean insisted on going to bed late – I needed to let her do it alone. The P of A had arranged a 'baby alarm' to connect her bedroom with my mine, by the time I was moving in full time.

Apart from the on-going writing and work, I needed to arrange, with the collaboration of the P of A and the Man with a Van, to pack up and move. I truly felt carried at this time, especially when I learned my sister was dying, and sent her a voice message for her daughter to play to her.

The week before I planned to move, I was informed by my niece and nephew, that my sister's funeral would be on **Monday 24th November.** Despite all my plans, bookings of trains and eventually a plane ticket it wasn't to be that I went to it. Even the direct flight from Edinburgh to Cardiff was eventually cancelled after waiting two hours for it to arrive and leave!!! I got all flight and train ticket money refunded! Although disappointed not to see my niece and nephew I was relieved as I was very tired.

Back to moving the flat. Despite physio, the right shoulder cuff damage was still very painful and meant I could not pack any books that were above waist height, and everything was very slow. But my dear 'treasure' who had helped me maintain order in the flat, came to help pack on agreed days,

Thursday 24 November 2022

the two men (with the van) and a young man from church gave me full-time help between them in order to pack up the flat. Glory to God.

The following day the men with the van moved everything to Jean's house.

Dear Reader – I do not deny it was difficult. A, when helping me pack on the Thursday had suggested I spend some time on the beach on the Friday when they were loading the van. Acknowledgement of loss is crucial for Spiritual well-being, but I needed to accept it!

Friday 25 November – On the beach by the flat...

I found myself speaking out loud while I was filming the waves:

> The sea will continue lapping –
> The waves breaking on the shore,
> The tide receding and coming back
> And flooding the places it had been before.
>
> And nothing can take away from me the Love of God
> And the waves of Life that lap on the shores of my heart;
> Nothing can take away the beauty and wonder of the
> Cross
> That gives me Life and allows me to live each brave new
> start.
>
> And I know that though I cannot see the path here,
> God knows, and I do not need to know the Way,
> But like these stones, stand in the beauty and wonder of
> Christ –
> And know that He is God; He is the Breaking of each Day.
>
> He is my Lord, and as these waves continue to lap,
> So His Life will beat in me to Eternity;
> Do I understand that? No. Do the stones understand? No!
> They accept the Word, the Grace of being in His
> Creativity.
>
> So standing to the Glory of God in praise and
> thanksgiving –
> With the stones I will praise His Name.
> And All manner of things will be well...
> All manner of things are well, and in Him I will remain.

I was comforted by filming the waves and by the words that had
come from my heart. Once the van and my car were loaded, we
drove into Edinburgh to Jean's. A was already shifting beds and
mattresses and emptying furniture from upstairs to make space

for mine when I arrived with my carload of bags.

Seeing Benefits for Jean

Jean was finally getting her old mattress (which had been on the upstairs bed) back onto her new bed downstairs, which she had been asking for since the new bed had been installed. Otherwise, we managed to keep the disturbance of all the moving apart from Jean as she was hard of hearing.

By that evening furniture was basically in the right places with book boxes mainly in the small front 'cell'. All the excess furniture of Jean's upstairs rooms had found space in the garage and made space for my needs. It took a few days for the dust to settle, and I was daily inspired to re-arrange what furniture I had to make an iconography and a 'kitchen' area in the large front bedroom. The backroom upstairs, which got sun in the morning and overlooked the garden, housed my computer desk and the simple cane chairs for contemplative prayer.

Over the next two weeks volunteers came from church for a morning or afternoon at a time to help unpack books in my 'cell' and into the iconography bookcase.

Very soon Jean became accustomed to having supper at 7pm, her chosen time, but I realized I could not go to Vespers at church if I didn't make other arrangements. I mentioned my desire/need and said we would try leaving her supper well wrapped but already plated. In fact, we didn't do this very often, but it worked well when we did.

Praying about my Role?

Jean was very happy to have a full-time carer at hand (and loved hearing footsteps upstairs), but I had never believed this caring was essentially what I was called to do. I really sensed I was there to strengthen her in faith and love and prepare her to let go in order to be ready to die, which she essentially wanted to do. Jean and I, with others, had long known each other as prayer partners, in prayer for renewal for ourselves, and for the church.

To begin with I was not very willing to challenge the way things were in the house – but as I got to know the care routine, and could find a way I could contribute, when necessary, I began to realise my limitations in terms of strength and care experience. I surrendered all to private prayer for her and the work of the Holy Spirit to prepare her for death.

She made it clear she did not want a commode, or wheelchair, so as her body weakened, she became more and more vulnerable to falls which she had had when living alone.

But my heart was filled with love and compassion, and when I suggested using a tea-towel as a sort of 'bib' to keep her clothes cleaner – she accepted it without argument…even asking the morning carer to put it on her for breakfast. While maintaining a clear respect for her integrity, I found tenderness pouring from me, as for a favourite child. God was loving her through me in new ways. Also, she was very grateful for all I, or the carers did – a new side of Jean.

I felt very privileged to do this work of love, and as I learned more of the things that would help her…. I gave more time when I could.

We knew she had had falls at night or evening -and with more help during the day there had not been any for a few weeks.

As Christmas approached, I asked Violet, another 'old prayer-friend' if she would be free to join us for Christmas. She was happy to do this, and she started to make food plans, though Jean was happy to stick with her regular frozen meals.

All Change

But two weeks before Christmas I got back from Church and heard her call for help from her downstairs bathroom. She needed help in getting her trousers pulled up. I left her re-established with her bedroom walker – which got her to the lobby. She got herself up the two steps in the lobby and changed to the walker she used in the kitchen and living room.

We had a brief discussion of what I might make for her, and I suggested a weak milky coffee as she didn't want tea. She set off with her walking frame towards her chair in the living room. My attention was on boiling the water and preparing the mug, when I heard a crash. Jean had fallen to her left, onto the small waste bins and banged her head against the garden-door and /or the second waste bin.

As I recall this situation now, I did all I could do to make her comfortable, and straightened her body so it could lie flat by pulling her by her jacket towards me and away from the door. She did not lose consciousness, and we called the emergency carers by pressing the buzzer alarm that she wore round her neck. I forget the exact time we waited for their arrival, but it was maybe 20 minutes or more. I got a cushion for her head and sat with her simply loving her.

I was very impressed by the 'rescue' people and their amazing means of raising fallen people safely and without undue stress on their own backs. Simple technology at its best! They very carefully got Jean vertical and walked her back to her chair with her walker.

I made Jean the rather overdue cup of weak-milky coffee and left her drinking it while I went to deliver and collect some writing (Book 2) that someone was editing for me. It was a quick exchange, so I quickly went to Cameron Toll to buy calendar presents for Christmas gifts. As I was walking back to the car my phone rang. It was the emergency team wanting to know if I was in the house as Jean had buzzed her buzzer. I told them I would be 10 minutes getting back and would buzz them when I knew what the situation was.

Jean had gone to the toilet and had fallen in the bathroom trying to restore her trousers. There was blood but it wasn't clear where it had come from. Again, I straightened Jean using her jacket to pull her body straight. The team came in about 30 minutes – and got Jean back to her chair – walking with her and her walker.

At that time, they said that if she fell again, I would need to call an ambulance because there may be an underlying problem which needed to be looked into. Jean told me she had nearly fallen a few days previously but fell against the table so had not gone down.

Needless to say, Jean was feeling very vulnerable – and so was I. I had no strength in my right arm as the torn cuff was still painful and no muscle had any strength! I felt, and was, powerless to help her physically. But I kept praying for the Lord to be with her.

Eventually around 7pm we sat together, and she ate her way through a small supper, and I had some food. About 8pm I went to go to my room and a friend rang me as I was going up the stairs. We started speaking and then I saw Jean was trying to ring me. I ended the conversation with the friend and went down to Jean.

She told me she needed to go to the toilet but felt very vulnerable and weak. I said that without a wheelchair or commode I was powerless, but we would try, and to keep holding on to the Strength of Christ as she walked with her walker.

As I reflect on this now, I realise that vulnerability stemmed from the damage to her brain, and although she managed the walk to the lobby area – she could not organise the motor control she had had in changing hands to the stair-rail etc and getting herself down the steps. Before I knew what was happening, she had fallen headfirst down the two steps and into the bottom walker taking up the floor space in the lobby.

We were both shocked; but again, I did what I could to disentangle her from the bottom walker and the other walker which had fallen on top of her with all its contents. I believed I couldn't straighten her, beyond removing the obstacles she had fallen into or brought on top of her, and when I spoke to the emergency team, or the ambulance – my concerns were about the angle she was lying – i.e., head downwards, face up.

The ambulance people were saying don't move her in case she's broken something…. The emergency team were reinforcing the need to get the ambulance – but that night there were very long waits. Again, I got a pillow for her head – and eventually something to cover her…and all I could do was comfort her – and silently pray. The ambulance did say – if there is any change then ring again.

The change came violently and suddenly when she started to vomit. Somehow God gave me grace to keep her nose airway clear – but I had no doubt that He was with her – and somehow she did not choke or drown. I felt I just had to let Him move through me ….and together, with the Holy Spirit controlling her, and me, she survived the first bout of vomiting when everything was against her survival. I phoned the ambulance again and she moved up the 'emergency' list.

I then had to find clean towels and a dry covering for the pillow. Eventually after the second bout of vomiting during which I forcibly moved her head sideways, I needed to ring L, a friend/carer of Jean who knew more about where towel stores were in the house.

By the time she had arrived, Jean had moved up the emergency list further, and the Emergency carers had agreed to come and get her onto the level to wait for the ambulance…but they had long waits too!

When L arrived, she realised I was in a state of shock … and she very gently found more towels and tidied up what she could to make Jean more comfortable. I am barely conscious of the next period of time…. Except I saw Jean was being cared for…with at least one more bout of vomiting.

The ambulance arrived after 10pm, before the emergency carers but interestingly the paramedics would have valued the equipment of the emergency care team to get Jean upright. But when the emergency carers arrived, they didn't want to 'tread on any toes': so, having established that the ambulance crew were present, they left without knowing they would have been valued!!

The paramedics were keen to know the 'facts', and L knew more about Jean's medications etc, though I could tell (probably incoherently) of the three falls of that afternoon/evening.

It was a relief to see the ambulance team checking Jean out – eventually getting her flat and into the ambulance where they did more tests. It was agreed that L would go with Jean to the hospital, as she knew more of her medications and history…and I would wait to hear from her in the morning…having cleared up in the house. In fact, L's husband came to join her at the hospital, so she was not left to face that alone.

I cleaned the bulk of the mess that night and put towels and pillowcases into the washing machine and left them on a hot wash. I don't remember getting into bed or falling asleep – but woke when I received a text around **7am December 12th 2022.**

I had got a text from L to ask me to find the text number of T (a Minister friend of Jean's) and to tell him if he wanted to see Jean, he probably needed to come today. At 7am I did not phone T, but I did go and find his phone number and sent it to L. After more sleep I phoned T about 9am, by which time L had been in touch with him, and he was going to go to see Jean.

Hospital Bedside

I got to the hospital about 11 in agreement with L, to take over 'being with Jean'. When I was on my own with her, I was led to pray for her and found myself 'laying hands' on her forehead; I felt the heat coming through my hand to her head. I do not normally either 'lay hands' on people or pray for healing, so I was surprised, but trusted God was in charge.

When I had been told there was bleeding in the brain, I had assumed it was at the back of the head where she had originally fallen onto the small compost / food waste bin in the kitchen. But later that day I heard more detail about the brain haemorrhage which was in the frontal lobe…where I had been praying.

Only God knows what healing He brought about through that prayer. She had been expected to die on Monday when they had seen the extent of haemorrhage…. hence the message to T. But everyone who came was praying for her…. And in some ways, she was clearly becoming more able to communicate through the week.

Comment

I had never experienced someone on 'End of Life care' which cuts out food and water…. but provides medication to alleviate pain, and distress. Increasingly Jean's mouth was very dry. To begin with she had refused water and moisture as if she had been Christ on the Cross; but she too went through 'thirst' and accepted the sponges dipped in water.

These were the things that occupied me when I was left alone with Jean between visitors – but I was concerned about Jean establishing contact with her family and forgiving them. It took till Thursday for me to ask KN, the Power of Attorney, to get in touch with her brother's family and invite them to send voice messages to me. Jean's niece sent a message – and I played it to Jean on the Thursday…. Clearly Jean recognized and appreciated the message. By late afternoon we had also played messages from her sister-in-law and her nephew with varying responses.

Jean had seen my computer on Thursday and clearly wanted something from it. I remembered that she used to Skype with her Chinese student/friend every week. They would pray together. I told her I would try and find Yin Chen. I sent messages to Violet to see if she knew anything about her contacts.

Friday 16 December 2022

Later that morning I played a second voice message from her sister-in-law, with whom she had spoken frequently on WhatsApp video calls. As I held my phone to her ear Jean reached to my hand and brought the phone in front of her face in order to 'see' S! I realised she wanted to have a video call with S and I sent a message asking if she could do a WhatsApp video call, not knowing what God had arranged!!

Within half an hour the nephew who was with Jean's sister-in-law visiting his father in a care home, had responded and Jean had about 20 minutes of interaction with her family. It included a declaration from her brother that he loved Jean. It was so healing for Jean to be present to her family and to actually have visual contact with her brother.

During that week, she also had visits from a number of people from her current church who all prayed for her, and many asked for her forgiveness for not visiting more. I felt so privileged to walk with Jean on this journey.

Division of time and Spiritual Support

Although I had spent Monday night with Jean, I came to see that I could not do this on a regular basis. I decided I would do 'days'…which is what I did. But Jean showed me a new awareness of 'Christ is with me'.

As I mentioned, when I first moved into Jean's house my spiritual Father had offered to come and pray for the house, for Jean and myself. During the prayers of blessing of the house and people, she asked questions about the sign of the Cross and what it was for and what it meant. I had said at one point that it was a comfort to re-affirm His Presence and declare my commitment to Him and His Cross.

While in hospital I would pray with and for Jean, but most

frequently silently, because I didn't want to interfere with what the Lord was doing with her. But one evening when I was about to leave and had prayed and affirmed that the Lord was with her, she made the sign of the cross with her right hand – in a very deliberate way. By then she was talking very little but spoke volumes in other ways. That evening I sensed her strength in His Presence.

However, on the Saturday evening I needed to go earlier than I had been, as I was trying to follow up contacts in relation to Yin Chen her Chinese friend, so I told her I had to go. As I always had at the house, I told her when I would be back – in this case - after church on Sunday. I affirmed that the Lord was with her. She 'told' me she was afraid. I Spiritually handed her to the Lord and told her she would NEVER be alone and both physically and Spiritually she was cared for. I knew I must TRUST God and His angels….and 'set my face like flint' (Isaiah 50:7) and go. I believe this was a turning point for Jean – in terms of letting go of earthly dependencies.

When I got back on the Sunday, the nurses told me she had had a very quiet restful night and was now sleeping peacefully. I went in without waking her up…and before I knew it, I was asleep. I woke up in time to see the nurse peering in to see if Jean was ok. I gave her the thumbs up – then wondered what I was to do. I started reading, then suddenly became aware of a tiny noise from Jean. I looked and her life had gone! In a tiny moment she had lost her signs of life. When I looked at the time it was 4.20pm. On the Friday I had sensed she would die at 4pm….. but not on Friday! In the mercy of God, he had delayed her passing for me to be awake. Glory to God.

I went to get the nurse, and together she did what was immediately necessary, and I prayed with many tears and thanksgiving to God for Jean's life. I phoned L who came when she could and found a favourite nightgown for the nurses to dress Jean in when they had washed her. L and I prayed over many facets of Jean's life while we waited in the quiet room, but when we went back into Jean's room, once she was washed, we both realised that the Spirit was no longer there. She died on the day of Resurrection to go with the Lord. Glory to God for His witness.

A day or so after Jean died, we did make contact with Yin Chen - who I invited for Christmas to help her come to some closure of their long and loving friendship in Christ. We spent Christmas Day at Violet's house, but Yin Chen needed time alone. So back at Jean's house, although I was in the house, Yin Chen was largely self-contained in the room downstairs, or out on many long walks. The Lord brought healing and great integration of her soul through the two weeks she had in Jean's house.

We had **an evening of thanksgiving for Jean** and each invitee sharing something of what Jean had meant for them. We did this largely because Yin Chen could not stay any longer to wait for the funeral or memorial service. So, we had our own memorial in the house, and all recalled the gatherings that Jean was instrumental in holding in her large sitting room, always to honour and build up Christ in each person.

Jean had been self-contained, but she had reached out to many – not least all the students she had taught as a Midwife, or as a university lecturer in Nursing. She had given accommodation to many students over the years, encouraging many in a living faith in Christ. She had been a member of many different churches, always seeking the life of the Holy Spirit, and somewhere where she could be enabled to hear. She herself served churches with her many books and writing and editing skills.

What Now?

Although we had known this would happen, I certainly wasn't prepared for it so soon. I think I was humanly in a state of shock for about 2 months. I was not in denial but waiting for God to open up a way. He had promised before I left Prestonpans that He would provide a flat for me, and so I focused on the work I

needed to do on-line and for Book 2, and on what KN needed
me to do to support him as Executor. I believed that God would
provide a flat for me at the right time.

Completing Book 2

One element of writing the book was overcoming my own
intransigence. I truly wanted the whole book to be a bearer of the
message and the gospel of Christ…showing the Height and
Depth and Length and Breadth of Christ's Love, including the
forgiveness and long-suffering, that He had enabled me to live in
service.

When it was read by others their feedback helped me recognize
that I needed to amend the 'voice' of the telling in places – in
order to be true to Him and my Inner Being. This delayed
publication as I re-wrote parts and had to wait for re-reading etc.
But I want to say that the Lord wanted certain elements of MY
acknowledgement of my sin in holding on to false gods, to be
clarified, as it is so crucial for the healing of broken hearts. While
we live with human fear and false gods we cannot LIVE for or
by Christ because we are controlled by fear of man, not Love for
God and mankind. All of this 'stretched my boundaries', and
indeed Christ was with me as my purposes became more purified
and pure of heart.

But along with Jean's funeral service, and her memorial service
which was a real witness to her Life for Christ, all things moved
along…….

And by **February 13 2023**

Book 2, 'Your Will Be Done: Beyond Powerlessness Fear – Life revealed in Love' was published on Amazon. We had an official Book Launch on Friday 17th February which was recorded.
The trials with this book were not over. I ordered 'author's copies' from Amazon and when they arrived, they were misprinted in that each page was 3" x5.5" instead of 6"x9" the size of the book!!

It took over 2 months and a lot of emails to get it back up as a printed book with the proper size pages. But it never really phased me…I just kept putting it in God's hands and got on with the next step.

And that was to at least start to think about moving and take the practical steps needed. I prayed for the next steps.

8

And know the love of Christ which passes knowledge; that you may be filled with all the fullness of God." (Eph. 3: 19)

In God alone I put my trust.

Thursday 23 February 2023

No day passes, when we surrender all to God, without a descent into hell, or a touch of heaven!! Life is like a theme of music with new developments of the major harmony which widen the whole picture yet bring focus to the next step.

So, it was as I opened my eyes to accept that maybe I needed to do something about being homeless. A soon-to-be homeless friend from church had been searching for some time and had sent me links to gain access to the forms needed to sign up for the Edinburgh Council lists. But before I did that, I Googled flats available for rent in EH16 and areas within access of the church.

When I saw one on Little Road, I went to have a look at the outside and then went online to find how to apply for it. I discovered it was a Housing Association mid-market rent property, and on the form, I had to say if I was anyone else's housing-lists. In completing their form and saving all the documents – I had indeed 'prepared the Way'.

This question about other lists, reminded me of Touchstone who I had rented from before. I still had the contact number of my old Housing Manager

Friday 24 February 2023

I rang her. By the grace of God, she answered, and I told her my
situation. By the end of the call, she had promised to send me
today's list of flats coming up for rent which she received each
Friday. She told me to tell her if any appealed to me, and she
would book me a viewing.

True to her word I received the letter and list and instructions of
what to do if any 'appealed'. I dutifully went through the
addresses trying to see where they were…. but one seemed to be
lost on the Google map. … I found myself responding:

Dear Karolina,
Many thanks for doing what you said.
Nothing immediately grabs me, **except maybe 4 Robin Place. I
will try and find it over the weekend and let you know if I am
interested in a viewing….'

** Here I was going to sign my name, but the Holy Spirit added
the rest!! So, I determined to go and look for it on Saturday
with my Godmother who lived within close walking distance.

Saturday 25 February.

The flat was in the community area of the Thistle Foundation in Craigmillar, Edinburgh. It wasn't easy to find the address – and we were initially pointed to a no 4 Chapel Court which was also empty. But eventually we found an empty flat 4 on Robin Place and found the back garden. We could see into the back living room through the locked gate. It was two bedroomed and would be less than I had been paying in Prestonpans. My Godmother was concerned it might be rather dark. But the day was rather dark so maybe it was not a real concern?

I was still doing on-line work when prompted, and I had been prompted to start making videos, which after prayer became clarified as 40 x two-minute Lenten videos with the title 'Journey Within'.

Monday 27 February

The first Day of Orthodox Lent, I made and posted the first Video, and I filled in the Application form for 4 Robin Place, using all the documents stored after applying for the Little Road flat! Truly this was a Lenten Journey.

I recognized eventually that the decision about this place was not mine, but the Lord's…and had already been made. But it took me time to recognize this, and I still thought I must apply to Ed-Index and to make myself officially 'homeless. I worried unduly when I had my 'Notice to Vacate' letter (from the PofA) to send to Ed.Index . I had applied, more in humility than a sense of need but it opened the door to uncertainty. Maybe Spiritually I needed to know the dreadful human vulnerability of the homeless, when they are powerless to make anything happen.

Wednesday 8 March 2023

In my powerlessness of 'not knowing', I was feeling separated from all good action. Yet I was prompted to phone the Touchstone Housing Manager who had been helping me and to whom I had sent the requisite application form and supporting documents on February 27th. I had heard nothing since I sent them.

I left a message on her phone, without a lot of hope that she would respond. But she did, and she told me my application for 4 Robin Place had been accepted by the letting team, but they hadn't got back to me with a date for viewing because they needed to wait for the flat's 'release' from the works team. She actually said, 'The flat is yours if you still want it after the viewing.' The flat was due to be released on Friday 10th March.

Thursday 9 March 2023

I got an email telling me of a viewing appointment on the following Tuesday, 14th March. Glory to God.

Tuesday 14 March 2023

I invited KN to come with me as he has an eye for detail, and I had been warned there was no second viewing prior to moving in – so I was armed with a tape measure and notebook to check out room sizes, etc. and a list of questions. He willingly came with me…and even on seeing the hallway and entrance, before I had got inside, he spoke to the young man taking me round, 'She'll take it'!! He told me this afterwards!!

It was far beyond expectations – though I had long ago given up going ahead of God. I had prayed to accept whatever I was being given with gratitude and humility. But I had no need of the prayer. And KN was a blessing in 'filling in the gaps' in the provision of the flat! There were no 'white goods' but KN insisted that I took what I needed from Jean's if I didn't have it myself. And 'we'd sort out' the cooker, because Jean had very ancient gas hob and separate ovens so there was a gap in supply!

I was never good at being assertive, but KN said I needed to ask the Housing Association that the back garden gate lock was renewed for safety at the back – aswell as pointing out various cracked or mal-functioning items in doors, or items in poor condition. The Housing manager taking us round noted these things down along with the date I would like to move in - March 29th.

Moving in Spirit and in Truth

I emailed the letting person saying I would like to accept the flat after the viewing. Then I needed to patiently wait for the machinations of an official email, then 'sign' a letter of agreement with all the rules and regulations and things that needed to be accepted. I so easily fall into self-interest and impatience! Lord have mercy.

Meanwhile I was continuing to keep order with what I could – juggling and releasing changing plans with my family and doing the Journey Within Videos which meant listening daily to what the Lord was releasing, building or affirming. I came to the decision that I would not try to complete Book 3 before Easter as the icon of Christ needed to be completed and posted before Easter, and I needed to handle many facets of moving. When I made the decision to delay the writing till Holy Week – giving myself two weeks to complete unpacking after the move, I felt a weight lifted from me.

So, before the moving date I focused on getting the icon completed, giving it time to dry too. It's always a joy to complete and send a commission.

'Do not be anxious'

Although I totally trusted that God was going to see this through, trials concerning if, and who, would be able to help me pack – gave me trials of doubt!

Yet on **Saturday 25th March**, after the Annunciation Liturgy, those who had volunteered the previous Sunday came to help, either by car with me, or in their own vehicles. We had a total of 6 people during that afternoon and early evening: packing books, crockery, food, bathroom 'stuff', cutlery, and gathering together miscellaneous items like extension leads that needed to be packed. One dear soul had brought his drill and wood working tools so took down shelves/shelving, removed curtain rails that were going and provided skilled help to complete the work needed. It was awesome to be so blessed. And all commented on what a blessing it was to work as a team. God truly works all things together for Good.

Monday 27 March 2023

We had a further three young men, packing up iconography materials, iconography books and more kitchen stuff from downstairs. Together we managed to clear most of the surfaces in the studio and kitchen areas of the upstairs 'flat'.

Tuesday 28 March 2023

One helper was not able to come, but the kind help of the sole volunteer completed the tasks that were crucial before the stuff was moved on the Wednesday!

Moving Days 29 - 31 of March 2023

KN had insisted that Jean's estate was to pay for moving because Jean would have wanted it. Glory to God. So, it was organized with A – the Man (+1) with the Van – that he would come on Wednesday and moved stuff across to the flat – probably two loads. My major concern was in 'arranging the furniture' in the studio/bedroom. I had measured and thought it would fit – but needed them to bring particular bits of furniture and the roll of lino in the first load. I loaded up the car the night before so when A was almost loaded up, I set off to the flat leaving A to finish off and join me. I needed to take photos of the 2 meters to send to the Electric and Gas supplier…. And wanted to put down a rug runner to save the carpet from the worst dirt!!

A and L did two runs of loading and unpacking, and left on Wednesday afternoon with a promise, as arranged, of being with me on Thursday 30th with a final load from Jean's house. Then they would give help to put up shelves, curtain rails etc, and Lm would help me unpack books. On Wednesday night I had agreed to hand over the car to my 'car-share family' for Thursday and it to be returned to Jean's on Friday.

Thursday 30 March 2023

Early, as promised a gas engineer came to fit the gas/electric cooker that I had bought from Gumtree. KN had come to witness the delivery while at Jean's and encouraged me to bargain the price down as it was not 'professionally cleaned' and he was not at peace. When I booked the re-fitting of the cooker for the flat, the plumbers had said I needed the Maker's instructions, which in fact KN was not able to find on-line. However the engineer who arrived to fit it on the 30th, was neither equipped with the right fittings, nor new hose that KN had requested… so no cooker was fitted that day.

(PS KN decided he would not pursue it further – but we would get a new one and get Currys to take away this old one. This new cooker was delivered and fitted 11th April).

Prayer continues….
Later that morning the Open-Reach engineer arrived to set up internet connections…and I thought I would be able to continue the videos despite a late start. But the only way I could manage to get the video onto the computer was through making a Zoom video!! For some reason the phone-recorded video would no longer transfer to the computer!! – I let go of the concern and prayed it would become clear.

I cleared and organized what I could to make space for more kitchen stuff and furniture when A came with a fresh load.

Dear Reader – Note God's mercy – later that day I saw some reference to 'low data mode/ON' on my phone… and eventually I found where this was and switched it off. The following day I was able to 'air drop' the video to the computer as I had before! NOTHING is impossible for God if we pray and trust.

Friday 31 March 2023

The 3rd Day of moving – Beyond all expectations, A and Lm arrived early at the flat to cut the hedge and lawn as they were both very overgrown. They did what they could, in the front and back garden then they drove (with me in the van too) to Jean's to meet up with KN. A and L were needed for some moving arranged by KN– giving me time to clean and tidy sufficiently to encourage Jean's cleaner who was coming for the last time that day. I also gathered up things forgotten and selected garden furniture and tools.

We returned to the flat with both van and car re-loaded…. And then unloaded – making the spare room into the overflow room!!

A and Lm gave their whole strength till 2pm to help me make sufficient order to be able to continue the processes of creating a place where I could pray, write and paint, and indeed live. They promised to return after a week away to complete the putting up of curtains, blinds etc.

'I will never Leave you or Forsake you' (Deuteronomy 31:6, quoted in Hebrews 13:5)

I was daily led to 'the next step' and focused on what I was given to do – gradually re-building a place to live, work and have my being.

One young man from church had volunteered to help me get and put up a 'garden mini shed'. It wasn't easy as we needed to attempt to level the ground through sharp sand and two paving slabs for the front corners. It was adequate rather than good and rain stopped 'play' finally when we were both exhausted. Yet with two other inputs over the next two days it was erected. Eventually even the pile of 'garden stuff' camping in the corner of the living room, could be off-loaded to the 'shed'!!

Monday 10 April 2023

But above all, because of the focus and prayer provided by the Videos, Monday of Holy week brought a further release of bitterness, following an awareness of the 'lack of blessing for women in the church'…on Sunday,. Yet God had prompted a male parishioner to come to me after the Liturgy and he told me of the blessings he had received through Book 2. God was affirming the work. - Video 37 on Monday emphasised that I must be obedient to God, not man, and I must speak the Truth in Love.….'

Tuesday 11 April 2023

Thus, I was able to re-commit to the writing of this book as I had promised.

I used morning service time to do the bulk of the writing, and also some evening services…. But always I was leaning on the Holy Spirit of Love and Truth.

I have been purified in very deep and challenging ways. Truth is not denial or suppression. To stand for Christ in Spirit and Truth means obedience to Grace, the Power of God alive through the Holy Spirit of Unity and Purpose. And this was what I needed to use in writing the Book – as a Child of God- owning His Life in and through me… Owning the healing of the Broken Heart – even as a work in progress.

This is a poem I wrote in December 1998 a year plus after moving to Kintyre in Scotland. It has both historic and prophetic elements. But it tells of God's gift in Healing the Broken Heart.

Her Silence Deafened Him

The soul sat in the carnage of a life.
Love crushed and trust shattered.
A broken heart* in desert confusion
Seeking to find what mattered.
And the silence deafened him.

In silence she trusted that help would come;
In silence she bore the desert ways.
In silence she forebore to complain
But sought to honour God in all her days.
And her silence deafened him.

In emptiness he sought knowledge,
In isolation he sought new friends;
In helplessness he tried the ways of the world,
And abandoned the heart to serve his own ends,
As her silence deafened him.

But he could not survive on will alone,
And the wearied-striving-warrior returned
To share the silence, emptiness and isolation
And seek with her where God's Heart burned -
And her silence filled him.

He found the desert ways bear fruit in season
As truth and love bring freedom from strife;
He found in the Arms of Love the reason
To celebrate the wonder of a life.

And in Silent Joy the soul lived, whole again.

*The 'heart' in biblical terms is the Inner Being which consists of heart (including emotions), mind and will – and connects to God's Heart and Spirit through His Spirit at work in and through us.

This second poem, now made into a song/hymn was written after some years going into the Dark Night of the Soul. I had reflected on the promises God made to the exiled Jews and the Nature of His Care, how it felt humanly and the Spiritual reality.

Finding Pearls in God's Care

In being led from slavery –
My God, I sense I do not live;
Yet find an inner bravery
The world can never give.

In the cloud in Desert waste
My God, I think I'll die of thirst;
Yet find the Living Water baste
The heart that did not trust.

In the shadow of Your wing
My God, life seems very dark;
Yet I find the Light that praises bring
And I hear your call apart.

In the palm of Your Hand
My God, it seems I cannot move;
Yet I discover inner land
Your Love and Grace to prove.

Chorus:
Oh Glory to God the Father,
And Praise to Christ to King,
In the Power of the Holy Spirit,
My Heart will ever sing.

In the quieting of Your Love
My God, I sense emptiness;
Yet find the oh-so-gentle Dove
Fills me with bounteousness.

In seeing the Promised Land
My God, I cannot find the Way;
Yet You take me by the hand
And give me strength to fight the fray.

As the apple of Your Eye
My God, it seems my heart will burst;
Yet knowing the Love of Heaven high
My soul will never thirst.

Chorus:
Oh Glory to God the Father,
And Praise to Christ to King,
In the Power of the Holy Spirit,
My Heart will ever sing.

When I wrote this, I knew I was 'inspired,' and although it is tied to Spirit and Truth, the last three verses were prophetic at that time. Now He is bringing them into being…and yet more to come!!

To live as a child of God is as St Paul said, constant dying, and being born again in the Holy Spirit of Christ. (2 Corinthians 4:10-11) As we grow in the Holy Spirit of Truth, and thus desire for God and His ways, it is as if we are 'hard-wired' to His Life and purposes. Some-one told me recently before I moved into this flat, that I would get a better connection to the Internet if I joined the router to the computer by cable. I guess this is what being hard wired to God is about. In what way am I living for His purposes, His energies?

How do I reflect the 'everywhere present' that we pray every day in the Trisagion prayers?

Misconnections brought to Light

I have been challenged further during the 40 days of Lent (not counting Sundays) to face hidden fear; denial and hatred of a part of myself; hatred of those in the church maintaining their own rules but who deny God's Love and Kingship in women surrendered to God, and alive in Christ and His Word; and my unwillingness to face the Holy Spirit of Truth in me when it 'rocked the boat', so I was guilty of disobedience to the Cross. None of these are pure before the Cross and the love of Christ.

I daily give the Lord my surrendered will so He can 'search my heart and find any wicked ways in me' (Psalm 139:23-24). So He did!! And even the horror of the hatred and powerlessness I felt one morning, was lifted through His mercy, as I owned this hatred, repented, surrendered my will and prayed, 'Lord I am willing to be willing to forgive'. Simply in turning to God with this, instead of hiding with the anger and shame, my heart was changed towards them. And later I realized it was all gone, and I was no longer ashamed of being a woman for Christ, nor had I anything but compassion and prayer for those that denied the truth of St Paul's statement: 'In Christ is neither male nor female, Greek nor Jew, slave nor free....'

Finding God's Purpose

Everyone who loves the Lord wants the security of knowing God's will.

He tells us, and has told me many times, 'Do justly, love mercy, and walk humbly with your God.'
How shall I come to understand the Lord and devote myself to the Most High God? Shall I reach Him with burnt offerings? with year-old calves? Will the Lord be pleased with thousands of rams? or with a myriad of streams of oil? Should I give my firstborn for my ungodliness, the fruit of my body for the sin of my soul? He has shown you, O man, what is good. Or what does the Lord seek from you but to do justly, and to love mercy, and to be ready to walk with the Lord your God?' (Micah 6:6-8)

And as the process of this flat unfolded I realized – this was no longer a question of my choice for this flat. He had told me He had a flat for me back in November when I gave notice on my old flat so I was free to move to be with Jean in her last days. Part of me totally trusted – the silent bit of me totally upheld by God and His purposes. But the 'rational mind' still felt I had to take responsibility etc…. until through His Light, I saw my arrogance. God had spoken 'Craigmillar' to me around the time Jean died, but I would have liked a miracle to make community at Jean's house. But I needed to let go MY understanding.

Dear Reader – when you look at your life, where do you have Peace and Life? For me it is when I am trusting the Spirit's prompting for what needs to be done for that day – building a pathway for tomorrow but only focusing on today– and I am not resisting with judgement or my ideas.

Maundy Thursday 13 April 2023.

Like today I knew I must get on with writing the book as my 'walk with Christ' for Holy Week, but also needed were a visit to a shop to buy eggs and onions, (for Pascha eggs) and re-visit to the chemist for completion of a prescription. These were completed, even to breaking my own rule, and getting enough eggs to contribute to those needed for the church people despite the rule in the shop because of apparent shortages of eggs.

When I got back to the flat, I felt prompted to go and ask a question of the Thistle Foundation Centre which I needed to do in order to send an email to the Housing Association re a bike-shed key. Not only was this done, and I ate a nut and fruit snack for breakfast, but I also sent the email re the bike-shed key to the Housing Association.

Dear Reader What I am trying to point out – to me as much as for you- the wholeness of God's concerns. He has put me in Craigmillar in this community of people of all nationalities, educational levels, and physical, mental and spiritual need. But I need to be willing to LISTEN to His Spirit moving me, to do His Will, without judging it as 'holy' or 'not holy'. Thus, I am blessed with His Peace and Love to give to others. But I need to be willing to LIVE here – so I joined the 'well-being' Centre while asking about a bike-shed key, to persevere with re-gaining strength in my right shoulder which was damaged in August last year. From no movement it has been gently restored to some movement and was able to complete the icon of Christ three weeks before Easter.

As dear Children of God, the JOY you will experience is in Christ; the Hope that is constant in your heart is in the Holy Spirit of Christ; and the Eternal Life is hidden in Christ in God. This is not fantasy, but solid foundation built on (I paraphrase) 'I believe in Jesus Christ, the Son of God, Saviour and Redeemer of the World.' And I believe He is with me and overcomes all darkness and the lies of Satan..'

I have nothing more to give you dear ones. This is the Truth I live out from day to day….and what Joy it is when I am blessed with a trial, to pray for others who are suffering and know that I am sharing in the purposes of Christ in God…. Bringing life to the helpless, Light to the blind, Hope to the hopeless – and love and friendship to the lost…. Praying for a Will for Good/God throughout the world.

PS. **What next?**

Strictly speaking I really don't know in tight detail. But His Spirit will never leave me, my Yes to His purposes does not go. And I want to share two words spoken to me during this period of Lent when asking God to take me deeper in purification.

One Sunday when I had come out of more denial of the pain of loss in relation to my life in the church, I had gone in faith to Liturgy. One of the key priests who works for and with the Archbishop was there. I was committing myself to every Word of the Liturgy – when suddenly I 'heard' in my Being,

> *'Tell the Church, "No amount of doing things 'exactly' takes the place of the real purpose of the Church in Christ, to seek and save the lost in Love. Evangelism is KEY to My Life.'*

There was no need for 'discernment' I sensed the Presence of the Father's Heart and Love. …. And then in the silence, I went back to listening to the Liturgy. Then a short while after I heard:

> *'Do a PhD: 'Don't Weep for Me, weep for yourselves.'*

I started thinking about this… but I gave it back to the Lord and completed focusing on the Liturgy.

But I sensed the Gift and purpose of God in these two happenings. My whole mission since coming back to the Church, has been to spread the Truth of God's Love and the Grace of

Christ for the weary and heavy laden. I have needed to receive for myself, as the greatest sinner and disbeliever of His Love. Only by letting go and falling with the Cross can it be received and bear fruit.

We have no strength or Love of our own. *'Not by might, nor by power, but by MY Spirit,* says the Lord.' (Zechariah 4:6)

And the PhD idea is a subject that God has pointed me to so many times over the years after finally accepting that maybe He does love women, and we were made in His image!! He led me to write about it and finally is encouraging me to accept the crosses I have been given as sharing in His life and death. Take up your Cross and walk.

After the Liturgy I walked through an 'open door' in as much as I went and sat by Fr T of the Archdiocese, who was sitting by himself. We discussed his work with the traumatized and I gave him Book 2 which discusses the issue more fully. I told him about the prophetic Word given me today, and in essence he agreed. May the Lord enable it to take root in His Heart... and the Church become alive in the Word and intention of saving souls.

When I mentioned the PhD to my Spiritual father, he mentioned someone who it would be useful to talk to. May the Lord open doorways for this to happen. For my 'Yes' to God, I am finding myself 'collecting' prophetic words from the Bible, as He draws me to them... and (miraculously) remembering where they are!!!

Dear Reader – I do not pretend that my brain works perfectly now, and the Holy Spirit has 'total control' of my Life. But I am saying that through replacing the 'trauma' responses, as they emerge, through the Holy Spirit, I face every waking day with Love and thanksgiving; with knowledge that nothing separates me from the Love of God; that I am living in His Grace and guidance.

I still have difficulty swallowing, or speaking if I am walking on new areas of communication. But I pray and surrender the moments to the Lord, and His Joy comes to me, as He embraces me in compassion and understanding for myself, and the other. I TRUST Him to guide and lead the conversation through the Holy Spirit of Love and respect with any social situation He has enabled.

I embrace my 'dis-abilities' with tenderness, not judgement, or denial, and praise God for seeing me through all those years of 'striving to be good enough'!!...when it was He who gave me new Life every time.

Put bluntly, I LOVE God the Father, Son and Holy Spirit...and so I have no fear for the future...even the potential difficulties of negotiating a PhD and a mode of communicating it. My background in the 'nature of knowledge' gives me a stepping-stone – but to be honest I rely on Christ's Word (paraphrase) 'Don't worry if you are called to speak before the authorities...the Holy Spirit will give you utterance.' (Mark 13:11)

I simply believe and trust...and feel my whole life has been leading to this death. I live for His purposes and will live to His praise and Glory whether I know it or not.

Glory to God in All things.

Your Life

YOU are the Truth of what
Holds me together,
Binds me in LOVE
To ALL humanity,
Purifies my soul to seek
Your purpose for my life -
And the secrets
You promise
That come through
The Treasures of Darkness.

This is Your Story
Hidden in me,
Redeeming the lost,
Carrying Your Spirit,
Upholding the blind,
Strengthening the weak-
You are God –
Giving Life to others-
Through me –
When I say 'Yes'.

Timing; Trust; Hope: Honesty; Purity; Love;
The Truth sets us Free. Amen
Indeed you Heal the Broken Hearted.

Dear Reader come with me...lets walk together in faith – each day taking up our 'trauma-brain' cross. Lets rejoice in He who suffered an unsettled childhood, a life hidden then made very public through God's purposes for His Love and Word; authorities threatening Him and hating His popularity, wisdom and healing; plots to kill Him; unjustly convicted; hated and spat upon, rejected and despised; the agony of the pain inflicted on the body, and the loss of His human life, on the Cross.
And He descended after death to witness to those in hell to give them hope through faith in Him.

And Jesus Christ who rose again gives Life to all who open their hearts to believe...day by day finding the glory of His Cross revealing new Life, Hope and Joy and carrying them forward in humility, Truth and Love in God's Purposes.

Amen

If you want to contact me, or be encouraged, try these links and I will respond -in Faith, Hope and Love –

https://linktr.ee/h.marina

Here you will find courses, videos, website, and Facebook pages. May you grow in courage and grace to seek for His Way, Truth and Life in and through you to the glory of God the Father, and the building of His Kingdom......that you may become fully human through Christ's Love.

Index of Poems

Printed in Great Britain
by Amazon

35767250R00078